Storage Units

How to Buy at Auction for Fun and Profit

Sharon Pereida

Blessings!
Sharon
Pereida

Storage Units

Published by:
Intermedia Publishing, Inc.
P.O. Box 2825
Peoria, Arizona 85380
www.intermediapub.com

ISBN 978-1-937654-34-4

Printed in the United States of America

CONTENTS

Acknowledgments

Thanks to the many thousands of customers who have looked at, touched, and finally bought the used merchandise I have sold over the many years of being in the secondhand business. I hope that your purchase was just what you needed and that you went away feeling your purchase price was a bargain.

Thanks as well to the self-storage industry that provides me with a decent living, an education on human nature, lots of hard work, fun, and so many trips to the dump.

A special acknowledgment to my friends and fellow auction buyers; Ed Z., Herb, Big Bill, Ron, Mike S., Hector, Keith, Sam, Al, Harry, and Chris. Each one has their own special auction secrets from storage that they could tell.

And finally, the most important thanks go to my family. Thanks especially to my youngest sister Shirley Dieckman who typed and encouraged and typed and prayed and typed and helped all along the way. My sisters, Shirley and Doris, and I go boldly before the throne of God who is our source and strength for … "With man this is impossible, but not with God; all things are possible with God." Mark 10:27 New King James Version

Introduction

The orange resale permit that hangs in my cluttered office has the date 9/79, which is more than thirty years ago and when I began selling secondhand items. My knowledge of selling secondhand items began many years before. My siblings and I are all baby boomers who grew up in rural Pennsylvania. We were very poor but didn't know it. We might have worn used clothing and ate government surplus food, but because of our mother's wonderful sense of humor we laughed a lot and had lots of fun growing up. Shopping secondhand stores was a way of life and I learned at a young age the value of secondhand.

Selling secondhand items is a big business here in Los Angeles where the weather is perfect. There are more than fifty swap meets and flea markets, many open every day, some only on the weekend. With few exceptions and restrictions you can sell almost anything at a swap meet, which is what I do!

We have all heard about someone who purchased a painting, vase, or other item for a nominal fee at a yard sale or garage sale, only to find out later that it was worth thousands of dollars. These stories inspire us to go looking for those treasures at yard sales, garage sales, estate sales, etc. There are shows on television now that are meant to entertain yet they are also inspiring people to look for treasures in the purchase of storage units.

Finding that one special item or making money in storage involves cash flow, being at the right place at the right time, lots of hard work, and luck, but it can be done. I have been buying storage and selling the contents for over twenty years. In those twenty years I have seen some amusing, exciting, and gross stuff, as well as, made a living at it. However, if you are not interested in making a living at it and you have lots of free time, you can do this for fun, while helping your favorite charity's thrift store.

In this book, I will give you the complete "How To" information including: buying units at auction, selling the contents for a profit, and some ways to avoid costly mistakes that can result in a loss. Throughout, I have also included **KEYS** that you need to keep in mind when you begin buying and selling storage units and their contents. In addition, I have included some of my own personal stories from storage unit buying that I think you will find both entertaining and informative.

CHAPTER 1

Before the Auction

Reasons Why Storage Units are Available:

The number one reason self-storage units are sold at auction is for failure to pay the rent. The contract that you sign when you place your personal or business items into storage will outline the payment agreement and your access to those items, this is a binding contract. If you don't pay your rent, the items that you have stored can be sold for the accumulated late rental charges. When the failure to pay is a result of bankruptcy, the unit may not go to auction for many years. Each state has statutes and/or codes that govern self-storage and when the storage facility can auction a unit, see www.storagelaws.net for the statute in your state.

Some of the other reasons for storage units to come up for auction are; the owner has died, the owner has moved without a forwarding address, or the credit card the owner has on file for payment has expired. All of these reasons result in non-payment. Occasionally, the owner may no longer want the items and/or moved out of state and has signed a release of ownership statement that allows the storage company to sell the unit at auction. The owner is still liable for the rent if the sale of the goods does not cover the amount due. If the unit sells for more than the amount due, some facilities refund the overage amounts.

Owners can be evicted from their storage unit for; sleeping, cooking, or living in the unit, interfering with or inconveniencing other tenants or management, and storing or using hazardous chemicals in their storage unit. If the owner is evicted from their storage unit and refuses to remove their goods, then it can be sold at auction.

Public Storage of Los Angeles waits a minimum of sixty-two days after non-payment of rent to sell a unit at auction. They follow strict legal guidelines for publishing and attempting to contact the previous owner before a sale. In many cases they will work with a tenant to resolve payment issues and allow the tenant to recover their goods. Public Storage of Los Angeles was approached by the television auction shows but declined making the following statement; "We are not in the auction business we're in the storage business." Many of the items in storage are the owner's cherished possessions and as one Public Storage manager told me, one of the saddest things for them was to see someone completely distraught over losing their unit at auction.

The final reason a storage unit comes to auction is it may be a "company unit." This unit belongs to the company and contains usable items from previously abandoned units that are accumulated over time until the unit is full and then put up for auction. These units will not be published and will be announced as a "company unit" at the time of the auction. **KEY:** A storage unit may be called a unit, a room, a locker, a container, or as my friend Big Bill says "a butt-kicker."

Reasons for Buying Storage Units:

Today the economy is different, if you depend on a regular paycheck and have a great job that's wonderful. In this new economy many members of the household must work to make ends meet. If one person in a two-family paycheck loses their job, it can be financially devastating. Add to that the high unemployment rate and finding another job is not accomplished as quickly as was in the past. Many who are currently unemployed and even those employed are looking for ways to enhance their income. Most business opportunities that offer start-up help, with few exceptions, require an initial investment of cash.

If you are struggling and have the time, a covered vehicle, and aren't afraid of hard work, you can make money buying storage units at auction with a small investment. There is a saying in Spanish "En gota por gota se llena el bote`," translated loosely it means "drip by drip your bucket will get full." I make money one dollar at a time. Patience and persistence are requirements for buying and selling storage unit contents. I see the same people at the auctions, week after week and our stories are the same. Only one storage buyer I know just bought a Mercedes and when I saw him last week and made a "Wow" statement at his purchase he said in reply, "Only fifty-six more payments."

The Bible says in Matthew 6:19 (Amplified Version), "Do not gather and heap up and store up for yourselves treasures on earth, where moth and rust and worm consume and destroy, and where thieves break through and steal." Many people and businesses store up stuff and then lose hope, money, and their possessions. I see sad lives depicted in lost storage units. Keep in mind your most valuable asset is your family and loved ones. As Suze Orman says; "People first, then money, then things."

Read this book to find out the "How" of storage unit buying. However, keep your attention on the benefits of the family and friends you have. Then by all means step into my world of clothing, junk, and any item imaginable, as you buy storage units at auction and then sell, donate, and recycle the items just for the joy of the find.

Where to Find Auctions:

All states have statutes that regulate the sale of abandoned and unpaid storage units, see the appendix for a website source to these statutes. One requirement of all states is that the storage facilities must advertise the upcoming auction of abandoned or unpaid storage units. You can find these auctions in various ways.

One way to find auctions is to subscribe to a local paper. Be sure to check your small local papers as well, ads in large papers can be expensive. Many storage facilities use smaller, more obscure papers. These papers survive financially by placing auction announcements and notices. Also, there are online sites that list auctions; see the appendix for a list of these websites.

Another way to find auctions is to just stop in at a storage facility near you and ask the property manager when the next auction is or where they advertise their auctions. **KEY:** Be respectful and polite to all property managers, you will be dealing with them if you buy a storage unit at their facility. Property managers usually know when they are having an upcoming auction and can give you the name of the auctioneer or company holding the auction. **KEY:** Remember that storage facilities are in the business of providing storage, not in the business of holding auctions.

If you know the auctioneer's name or company you can call their office or look them up online. Online auction schedules will be posted, but be aware that cancellations occur regularly because tenants pay back rent, so check these sites just prior to attending the auction. An auction may be cancelled right up until the last moment because the owner has paid. Even as the auction is going on the owner may come and pay, or pay online, and the auction bid will be cancelled. There are examples of what a newspaper auction listing looks like in the appendix. Some buyers look to see the owners' names that are published and will do online searches of their name. This may help them decide what to bid at the auction, or what might be in the storage unit if they are a musician, artist, or famous. This can be time-consuming, yet if you have the time then by all means do it.

Choose a facility close by you to attend your first auction. Your first experience for an auction should be only as an observer. This will give you a feel for what to expect when you are there as a buyer. Be on time; or even early, go to the property manager, whom you may have met earlier, and explain that you are only there to observe. They may still require you to sign in even as an observer. **KEY:** When the auction starts remember you are not there to bid, so limit your hand movements and gestures.

Tools:

LOCKS—buy several locks with keys, combination locks are too time consuming to unlock so get a lock with keys. The dollar store has acceptable locks but don't buy the smallest ones, 2x2 is a nice sized lock. Unpack them; try the keys in the lock so you know they work, and mark the lock and key with matching numbers or letters; nail polish works best for this or permanent markers. Then when you buy a unit you will be ready with your lock and can move with the auction group to the next unit for sale. They will not wait for you if you have to find and mark your lock. Also, when you return to the unit to empty it out the key will be easy to find. **KEY:** Some buyers have multi-locks with all the same key, this is expensive and will reduce your profit.

Buying inexpensive locks reduces the cost if you lose your key or get to the unit and have forgotten your key, it will be much easier to cut your lock then go back to get it, especially when you have others with you to help you. **KEY:** Cutting a lock is frowned on by the storage facilities and is only done in an emergency, so don't lose your keys.

Entering a storage facility with a bolt cutter is NOT a good idea. You will be identified as a possible thief looking to cut some random unit's lock. You must advise the property manager of your intent, show them proof of ownership, and give your reason for having to cut the lock. Some property managers will only allow a lock to be cut with their equipment and may charge you up to $15.00, another good reason not to lose your keys.

FLASHLIGHT—Almost any large flashlight will work, make sure it has a bright beam. You may not need to use it at an auction or may need it for every unit. The hallways in some storage facilities are dark and most units do not have their own light. You will use the flashlight to shine further into the unit to help see what is there. If there are boxes you want to be able to see what is written on them, where did they buy their shoes, is the unit full of furniture, or is there a large rolling toolbox hidden in the back. **KEY:** Remember you are not allowed to touch anything in the room and may have only one to two minutes to decide what you see of value and how much you are willing to pay. A good flashlight is invaluable.

CASH—Remember you are going to the auction to make money, bring the amount of cash you are willing to gamble. When they begin the bidding always remember what you have on hand and bid with that in mind. Professional auctioneers are trained to draw out a bid, so don't get caught up in the moment and overbid. You cannot leave and go to the bank to get more cash. There are a few storage facilities that allow payment with debit/credit cards and very few accept personal checks.

Many storage facilities require a cleaning deposit; this will be in addition to your unit's cost. The deposit can be $20.00 to $200.00 or more. Recently, more costly deposits are being required if you are not a regular buyer. The reason for this is because there are more new buyers who open their unit, spend time searching through the unit, walk away disappointed taking only a few items of value and leaving the unit tossed about forfeiting their deposit but leaving the property manager and/or company to remove and dispose of what is left. **KEY:** In some situations there is no cleaning deposit required; however, you will only be able to buy ONCE at these facilities if you leave the unit dirty.

RESALE PERMIT—You will have to pay state sales tax in California on your purchase unless you have a resale permit. A resale permit says that you have a valid business address in California and will collect sales tax on any items that you sell. You are not required to have a resale permit but will have to pay sales tax at 8.75 percent (currently in L.A.).

The California state board of equalization has forms that you can copy and print at www.boe.ca.gov/pdf/boe230pdf. Other states have similar resale taxes forms and can be found on the government pages at the business portal under sales tax information. Print out these forms and have multiple copies available when you go to the auction to purchase a unit. Remember to check the website listed in the appendix for the statutes governing storage facilities in your state.

CHAPTER 2

During the Auction

When You Arrive at the Auction:

Now that you have gone as an observer and have a feel for what happens you can choose an auction at a facility near you to attend. On the day of the auction be ten to fifteen minutes early, auctions do not wait for late comers under any circumstances. Most auctions require you to sign in on a sheet of paper, put your phone number down, and possibly other information, such as, an address or driver's license number if you plan on buying. See the appendix for an example of an auction sign-in sheet. You may note at this time, as when you were there observing, that there were others waiting for the sale to begin, some regulars talking together, and some buyers standing alone. A buyer friend of mine once told me, "I'm your friend 'til the doors go up and then it is all business." Keep in mind you are the competition!

You are ready for the auction to begin, you have your tools and know your cash limit. When the auctioneer arrives there is a certain amount of paperwork that they must complete before the auction begins. If the auctioneer is on time and the paperwork is finished, then the sale will begin, usually on time.

One thing you might note before the auction begins is that instead of the ten or twelve units listed in the paper for auction, there are only one or two for sale. or maybe none so the sale is cancelled. Remember, storage facilities are in the business of providing storage space, not in auctioning people's personal belongs.

On a few occasions I have seen the owner or his/her's representative attend the auction to try and buy back their items at the auction. When they cry, plead, and appear sincere about wanting their unit back many regulars let them bid low to get it back. If you are a new bidder be aware what is happening and follow the regulars' lead in this situation. Don't drive the price up for the owner. When the owner is angry and rude to the bidders, the opposite happens, the owner will not be able to outbid the regulars. **KEY:** How you treat others in any aspect of life is how they will treat you.

Bidding:

Now the auction begins; you have signed in and have your tools ready. Follow the group; usually it's the man with the clipboard as you go to the first unit for sale. The auctioneer will give a short speech about turning in personals, not touching anything inside the unit, whether there is a cleaning deposit on the unit, and how much time you have to clean it out. If the unit is very large and full you may be able to have a few extra days to clean out the unit, this will be announced or you can ask later.

In some facilities, when you arrive at the unit door the original owners' lock will be clipped, drilled, or cut off. At other units the locks may have already been cut off, photos have been taken, and the lock has been replaced with a company lock along with a possible company seal.

Once the lock is removed the door goes up or to one side. There may be light or it may be packed to the door with a mattress covering the opening. You will bid on what you see, and gamble on what you don't. Auctioneers are professionals for the most part and many buyers are regulars who own thrift stores, used furniture stores, or sell at swap meets. Some buy to make a quick turn-over on high ticket items, while others sell on craigslist, eBay, or at a yard/estate sale. These regular buyers are good at evaluating what they see.

When you think of bidding also consider the location of the unit; the work involved emptying it will be important to your profit margin and to yourself. If you buy a unit for $25.00 and think of the great buy, you need to think about the labor involved. If the unit is upstairs, down the hall, and the facility only has a Big Jim fork lift to get it down. Well, the Big Jim forklift only has a 3x4 space to fill before you can send merchandise down. Then you have to walk down the stairs and unload before sending the forklift back up, while you climb back up the stairs. You get the picture of the labor involved. The easiest units are the ones that are "drive-up." These are units where you can drive your vehicle into the facility and put it right next to the door while you load. I have included a map of a facility with more than one floor in the appendix. Note the number of drive-up units and the location of the elevator.

Everyone has a minute to stand in front of the unit and look in, some units are neat, some horribly messy, some may have one suitcase, or be packed completely to the door with nice clean boxes or wrapped furniture. Most of the time you are gambling on there being things of value in the unit you cannot see. **KEY:** Bid on what you can see!! Boxes that say "grandma's crystal" or "camera gear" or "toys" may be what they have inside, but a flat panel TV box or apple laptop box may hold some household items that fit better in this box that the owner found behind an electronics' store. Boxes that are all the same and appear factory sealed could be new toy items, electronics, or maybe just a group of new parts for a factory assembly. Twice I have had someone's new CD; 10,000 copies that never made it to market because it wasn't as popular as the artist expected it to be. This buying is a real gamble and I have seen the $5.00 unit hold $7,500.00 in merchandise or jewelry and the $4,500.00 unit hold an entire dumpster of trash inside clean totes and/or boxes. I rarely gamble more than $500.00 and the most I have ever paid was $750.00. There are some buyers who regularly spend thousands of dollars. **KEY:** If you are just starting out, BEWARE and start slow.

Once you have had your minute or two to look, add up what you see and what you think you will get for it, quickly make a decision and settle on an amount you will pay. Keep that amount in mind and stay $50.00 under or over that amount. Don't forget you will need additional cash for the cleaning deposit and sales taxes. If you start the bid you will have the auctioneer's attention, but it's alright if you want to jump into the bidding as it slows down or nears the end. Don't look to see who is bidding against you, it doesn't matter. It should be just you and the auctioneer. Some buyers will walk away as soon as they look inside because they are not interested. Crowds are larger these days because of the entertaining TV shows, because of this you could be bidding against one or even ten others.

The bidding might start at $5.00, or maybe at $500.00. Most units sell between these two amounts. The professional auctioneers are quick to see bidder gestures. Some auctions hand out paper numbers so you can hold up your number to bid, if not, and you want to make a bid, raise your hand or get the auctioneer's attention by saying ten, fifty, or what you would like to bid. Remember, when the bidding starts keep within your willingness to pay and the cash you have on hand. **KEY:** Do not get caught up! Some are professional auctioneers who want to drive the price up.

Now it is Yours:

If you have made your last bid according to your cash reserve and no one out-bids you, the auctioneer will say, "Sold!" They will either close the door or expect you to do it and place your lock on it. Oops, you forgot your locks or, you bought five units and only have four locks. You may ask the property manager to put a company lock on the unit. They will do it, but when you return to remove the contents you will have to contact them prior to removing the contents. After the lock is on they will ask your name and record it on their paperwork. **KEY:** Make a mental note of where it is located, mark the unit number down or mark it on the facilities' map you may have been given. You could leave now, but the property manager will wait until the auction is complete before processing you. Observing the rest of the auction is a way to learn more and also lets you see what else was for sale. The main advantage of going back to the office is being the first in line to pay. Occasionally, there are two property managers available and you can pay quickly and leave.

CHAPTER 3

After the Auction

Paying:

At the end of the auction all buyers head back to the office to pay. It is cash only unless determined prior to the sale that the facility will take a debit card. You may have to again add your name, address, and phone number to the buyer information. If other units were sold and another bidder is ahead of you, wait unless the auctioneer has enough space to help more than one person at a time. Remember, on occasion the original owner of the storage unit will have come and paid back rent during the auction and you will not own the unit.

When the auctioneer is back in the office with your paperwork glance at it to be sure it has the right unit number that you bought and recorded. They will fill out a deposit request (or not) and ask for your money. An example: your winning bid was $85.00 for the unit, plus 8 percent sales tax (if you don't have a resale permit yet) and a $40.00 cleaning deposit would bring your total to $131.80. After you pay they will give you a receipt, at that time request a gate code to enter the facility.

Paperwork:

There are four very important reasons to keep your receipt or receipts: First, write the gate code or access codes on the receipt. Today most storage facilities are protected by security gates and security access even in elevators and passage doors. **KEY:** A code for the third floor will only have access to the third floor. There are some access doors that have access codes with a magnetic door holder with a timer on it. You can open the door, set the timer, and a magnetic catch will hold it open usually for no more than five minutes. The access code they give you is only good for the twenty-four to forty-eight hours that they give you to pick up the contents of your unit. If you can pick up the unit right away you may not need a code. Some storage facilities will not give you or the regular buyers a temporary access code, just be respectful of their rules and move on. You may be subject to reduced access hours or stuck inside a gate until the property manager is finished with a customer or lunch. Again, be courteous to the property manager, they are the boss of their facility most of the time and you may need them to help you at some point. I have included a receipt copy in the appendix.

Second, the receipt helps you know what unit you purchased; was it A13 or E67? It is much easier to find your unit if you know what the number is. I suggested earlier that you write down the location of the unit; was it upstairs, at the end of the hallway, or a drive up? The receipt will at least give you the number.

Third, you need your receipt to get your cleaning deposit back after you have cleaned out the unit. They may not have asked for a cleaning deposit because you are a regular buyer and are known for leaving the units clean. However, most first-time buyers will be required to pay a deposit.

Fourth, you will need your receipt to keep track of your cost and for tax purposes. Maybe you plan on making this a business or you want to build up an already existing business. You will need to keep track of how much this merchandise cost you. Keep a folder or large envelope, whichever works for you, in your vehicle to hold the receipts and empty the folder each month. You should also keep your gas receipts, tool purchase receipts, record of vehicle maintenance and upkeep, and any supplies you purchase to help with cleaning. This is only a partial list of receipts you will need for tax purposes that are expenses incurred as part of your unit purchase, consult your tax accountant for a more complete list.

Previous Owner Issues:

Most storage facilities require you to return personals to the office for the original tenant. Personals include but are not limited to: photos, income tax forms, birth certificates, passports, cremated remains, etc. These personal items should be placed in a box or boxes, marked with the unit number and name (if you know it), and returned to the office. It is possible that the property manager would allow you to leave personals inside the empty unit. **KEY:** Do this only with permission. There can be very few personal items in a unit or several boxes of personal items the owner wants back. Occasionally, the original owner will simply request only specific items be returned.

If the owner of the unit calls the facility because they forgot it was the day of the auction, or they didn't have enough money to pay back rent but they want to try and buy the unit back from whom ever purchased it, the storage facility will NOT give them your number, but will give you (the buyer) their number to call. You as the buyer are not obligated to contact the owner. The owner is at your mercy and some buyers never sell the items back. Other buyers will sell some or all items back if the profit margin is good.

If you decide to contact the previous owner there are a few things to remember. One, they do not know how much you paid for the unit; two, they do not know your number so if you call them, be sure to block your phone number, and third, keep in mind you are not obligated to return the items. People can be really attached to their "stuff." Recently, a man whose stuff I bought offered me less than I paid to get his things back. I didn't sell it back to him but made a special effort to return his personal photos and paperwork.

Some, but not many, storage facilities do not want any personal items back. They want you to take everything with you when you clean it out. It is very sad to dispose of someone's personal photos and papers. More than once I have tried to find people to return their personal items. I have used social media sites and even their own personal paperwork to find them, but could not locate them.

A word of caution, about eight years ago I encountered a real problem owner who somehow found out that I owned a thrift store and came by the store where she began screaming at me until I had to call the police. She followed me to a local swap meet, where she screamed that I was selling her underwear. She was truly obsessed with her stuff, just common household goods and clothing that had been in storage more than a year. She literally stalked me for six months and even turned up at my church where she told my pastor that I was a thief. The final straw for me was when she arrived at my home and frightened my thirteen-year- old daughter. **KEY:** Use caution when contacting the previous owner!

CHAPTER 4

Cleaning the Unit Out

Tools:

VEHICLE—Make sure you take a reliable vehicle to empty your unit, either a truck, van, or a couple of cars will do. If you have an open pick-up keep a tie down tarp handy in case of rain and also some rope. I use rope in a twenty-five to forty-foot piece and not the black plastic kind because it stretches too much. Never tie a knot in your rope; knots are hard to pull through a loop or behind a refrigerator. Tie down your rope in a corner first to secure it and leave the long end free and accessible.

I own a sixteen-foot Isuzu box truck with a lift gate, there is rarely anything that I cannot pick up. On occasions, I have to rent a truck. When I do I rent from Budget. Remember that renting trucks cuts into the profit, but it may be necessary when maintenance is required on your vehicle or when you have purchased a unit that contains more items then your vehicle can carry. Avoid renting trucks on or near the first of the month, many people are moving and there are fewer options for rent. The bargain times for renting a vehicle are during the middle of the month.

DOLLY, HAND TRUCK, OR CART—I use a sturdy dolly that does not have inflatable wheels that go flat. A great dolly is the Yeats aluminum dolly with a strap, but almost any sturdy dolly will work. For heavy awkward items, like large furniture pieces but not appliances, use a four- wheel flat dolly, these are easily slid under one end of the item and then you can easily roll the item. Do not buy the cheapest one; the wheels will give out quickly. **KEY:** Don't use cheap lightweight dollies of any kind as they will cost you more in the long run.

Most storage facilities will let you use their carts, but you will need to leave your driver's license, then they will give you the key to unlock it. Some facilities have unlocked carts you can use. Carts help if it is a small unit, you can usually unload in two cartloads.

PLASTIC BAGS—Be sure to buy the thirty-three gallon bags that are over 1.3 mil thick, 100 per box because household trash bags are just not that strong. Usually, a unit has loose or scattered items of trash that will not break through a thick bag either, unless there is broken glass; use a box for trash with broken glass. At times, I have been emptying a unit and needed more boxes. I found that even books can be loaded into a strong bag. Staying with the thirty-three gallon size bag usually will

assure you that you can carry it; anything larger that you fill, you will not be able to carry. **KEY:** To separate and sort bags of trash from other bagged items, just tie a piece of paper (trash) to the top of the bag so you can identify the bags of trash without opening them later.

GLOVES: I rarely wear gloves unless I am loading wood pieces. One of the girls who works with me wears medical type gloves all the time. If you feel things are too dirty or dangerous, then by all means wear gloves. The dollar store has leather work gloves and plastic gloves in more than a few styles.

MASKS: Keep dust masks in your vehicle in case you feel you need them. Storage units can be and usually are very dusty. If you have allergies or respiratory problems, by all means use them.

MARKERS: A sharpie or heavy duty marker is another good item to have with you when you go to pick up your unit. Use them to clearly mark the personal item boxes to be returned with the unit number and for marking your own boxes with; fragile, sell, donate, etc., this will save you time later.

BOX CUTTER: Use a box cutter to open sealed boxes, cut away packing material and for any other uses as needed during the cleaning out process.

BROOM AND DUST PAN: As I mentioned earlier, you must clean up the unit. Paper scraps, paper clips, broken glass, and any other small items should be swept up and removed. Any small, inexpensive broom will work and thin cardboard or paper can be used if you don't have a dust pan.

HELP: Removing the contents of a storage unit is hard work; having help makes the work easier and quicker. I have two helpers I use for picking up storage contents. We work together well and work fast. Your help should be honest and willing to work at random times. Large furniture items almost always require assistance to load, especially for balance, use help so you don't hurt yourself. Remember, paid helpers cut into your profit margin but can really save you time and personal wear and tear. If your business is a family project everyone can participate and realize the profits. All of my children have helped me at one time or another and each has a regular job now! **KEY:** This work is not for everyone.

WATER AND SNACKS: Storage units can be very hot and the work hard. Make sure you have a good supply of water for yourself and anyone helping you. This is very important during the warmer months of the year because most storage units are not air conditioned. Also, it is good to have snacks, such as, granola bars, string cheese, or fruit available if it takes longer than expected to clean out the unit you will have a source of energy to help you keep going.

When and Where to Sort:

Now that you have paid and have your receipt, you must decide where and when you can sort the items in the unit you have purchased. Do you have a vehicle with you that will hold all the items or are you going to have to return to clean the unit out and sort the items? There are two methods to clean out a unit.

First, buyers who buy a lot and have a warehouse or retail store, empty everything at once, packing as quickly as possible to take all items to their own warehouse or store to sort and separate. One reason for doing this is to finish the unit, pick up the deposit, and go on to the next unit as quickly as possible. Maybe rain is forecast for the next day or the facility may be closing or have shortened hours because of the weekend or holiday. Another reason could be that help is available after the auction to load up. If you have a place large enough to hold the stuff from the unit and a vehicle that can hold it all, you may want to load it up and go to your own place to sort and separate the unit contents.

The second option is on-site sorting. Take your cart or dolly, plastic bags, gloves if you need or want them, and your key to the unit. Open the door, size it up, and ask yourself the following questions before you begin: Will it all fit in the vehicle I have with me? Is there furniture and appliances? Are there lots of boxes in front? Is it a real mess? Are you prepared to sort? Do you have your box cutters and some big boxes? Do you have the time?

If your unit is in a hallway, through an outside door, you will usually find a timed light switch at either end of the hallway. If there is not a switch or button, there may be a motion detector switch that turns on the light, simple movement will turn it on. If the main hallway lights go off, it will be a matter of turning on the timer again or moving around outside the unit to activate the switch.

Once you decide to go ahead and load up and do on-site sorting, I begin by loading up the large bulky items first if they are accessible. Open boxes as you go starting with the closest ones in the front. Usually, whoever packed things put like items together i.e. kitchen ware, candles, etc. Maybe the boxes are marked on the outside, but do not assume this is what is in the box, always look. I found silver flatware in a box marked "vacuum parts." This IS the fun part of buying storage units, it is almost like Christmas. You are opening boxes that are not wrapped but that hold someone's great possession or maybe not. I am still surprised to see what items people pay to store in storage.

Bulky items like clothing, loose medium-sized items like toys or pillows can be stuffed in plastic bags and loaded into your vehicle easily. Save empty boxes or bags aside for trash you may (and will) find. If and when you encounter family pictures or papers, set them aside to return to the manager's office on the way out, this is much easier now than coming back later.

Most things you find will have value to some degree, unless you get a unit that belonged to a homeless person or a pack rat (hoarder), this is when you need the mask.

Move aside your small items and boxes while you load the larger things then place your smaller items in and pack your plastic bags around them. Packing is much like the game of Tetras except you go from larger items to smaller. **KEY:** Keep aside higher "get your money back" items as you load.

Cleaning:

Once the unit is empty, pick up all loose paper and anything else on the floor that may be trash, including the previous owner's old destroyed lock. Getting your deposit back depends on leaving the unit clear and clean. If you find upset soap powder, broken glass, nails, etc. you will be required to sweep and clean these items up. If no deposit was required you still need to clear and clean the unit of everything. You can be banned from facilities and auctions if you leave trash behind. You will definitely be banned from any auctions at the storage facility where you left a mess behind. **KEY:** Very few of the storage facilities allow you to use their trash cans, if they do let you use their dumpster, do not abuse this privilege by overloading it.

Now you have all the items in your vehicle and are headed out the gate. Most offices are outside the gate so park and let the property manager know that the unit is empty and you have removed your lock. Bring in the boxes of personal items you are returning, these should be clearly marked with the unit number and name, if you know it, or leave them in the storage unit as previously arranged. You can keep the photo frames if you want to spend the time to remove the pictures. I usually leave the photos in the frames. The property manager will usually always check the unit to see if it is clean. Then he will return your cleaning deposit if there was one.

CHAPTER 5

Sorting

How you sort can make a big difference on how much you make on your investment. Just going through and picking out the so-called valuable items, i.e. electronics, jewelry, watches, cameras, and tools should give you the main return on your investment. However, the other items can also help with your profit and serve a greater good for others and for the earth as you recycle and donate.

The one main thing that you hope to do with all the stuff in your storage unit purchase is to get your investment back and make a profit. You need to know right up front that not every storage unit makes a profit, some units will be losers. If you remember that almost everything has value you are more likely to make a profit or at least break even.

In this chapter I will cover five of the six areas you need to keep in mind while sorting the items from your storage unit. Because selling is your main purpose for buying a storage unit at auction I have dedicated all of chapter 6 to an alphabetical listing of categories concerning selling and have included some of my own selling experiences.

Keep:

In almost every unit there will be items that you can use and may want to keep. Have a separate place to set these items aside as you sort. Some of these items can include: postage stamps, envelopes, packing tape, general office supplies, new journals, cleaning supplies, laundry supplies, unopened soap, paper products—toilet paper, paper towels etc.

BEWARE of two things, first, of keeping too much. At the moment of this writing I have two large trucks full, a storage unit of my own (at $183.00 per month) and one spare bedroom in my house half full of “keep” items. Many items are goods to be sold at a later specialty flea market and some items are for eBay/half.com sales. Accumulating items from storage has been a vulnerability for me. My children have accused me of being a borderline hoarder. Monitor closely your reserve items or soon you may need a storage unit of your own. Many of my family members call me when they need something and I file a mental note to watch for this item or items knowing I will have a sale for sure. .

The second thing to beware of is BUGS. Examine the items in the storage unit that you are considering for home use or future sales. Many times the storage unit owner may have moved from a residence that was infested with roaches. Do not use the cardboard boxes from this unit for your selected “keep” items or you will be inviting unwanted visitors to your home. Although the storage facilities spray regularly and fumigate for pests, many bugs can survive six to twelve months in storage. **KEY:** Use consideration when selling these items, it is better to take a loss than to provoke a customer.

Of course, you will keep any loose change you find in purses, pockets, piggybanks, and sometimes cans of change; even pennies add up. Going to change counting machines costs money, so don’t do it. You can start a family change bank for a special vacation or purchase. You can roll these coins easily using plastic measures purchased at an office supply store. These make rolling coins fun and an easy family project.

You can keep new gift sets, perfume, toys, and games as gifts for friends and family. You can also find gift cards or certificates that people have put in a drawer or envelope and then forgotten about. These make great gifts for you to give or keep for yourself. One great shopping spree that I had involved a $203.00 gift card from Wal-mart. I checked the amount by phone and then in the store before I filled my basket!

Recycle:

Since living in California and specifically Los Angeles, I have found plenty of places to recycle most anything. Wire, metal, motors, computer cards, electronic equipment, paper, and some cell phones can all be recycled. I use SA Recycling for metals. General scrap metal or tin pays $175.00 per ton which is 2,250 pounds, gross weight. This metal can be found on: washers, dryers, other appliances, table bases, wagons etc. Because many times there is plastic, upholstery, or wood trim on your metal and to avoid time consuming metal cleaning they will deduct 250 pounds from your total. If you have iron car parts, brake parts, and other solid heavy metals the price is higher per ton. Ask the spotter or yard man to give you the best price.

The best copper insulated wire pays $1.45 per pound today, October 2011, and copper that is clean, unpainted, and unsoldered pays $3.00 per pound. Other current prices are motors which pay .25 cents per pound, and yellow brass which pays $1.80 per pound. See the receipt in the paperwork section of the appendix.

Computer cards have particles of gold and can be recycled for about $3.00 per pound. You will have to search for the best paying recycler near you by calling around or look online. Electronics and older computers have a recycling status that pays as well. If you have time and space, dismantle metal items to maximize profits.

Paper has recycling value too. Today's price for mixed paper in my area is $80 per ton. Mixed includes old paper files, file folders, books, and catalogs. The closer you are to downtown

L.A. or a port area the higher the payment for paper. White only ledger paper, without post-it notes or other color tabs, pays $180.00 per ton. It doesn't take much paper to make a ton.

Donate:

Donate children's books and plain paper you won't use to your local grade school. They are delighted to have it and if your local school has a parent room, enlist a parent or two to pick it up. Ask them what they need. Pencils, pens, markers, crayons, and folders are plentiful in storage units so donate them. Everyone will appreciate it.

Donate clothing and socks that you don't want to local drug or alcohol rehabilitation facilities or battered women's shelters. Most accept blankets and other bedding as well. Basically, you can donate to any of your favorite charities, just be respectful and don't just dump junk on them. **KEY:** Make sure what you donate is clean or new and free of bugs.

Trash/Hazardous Waste:

Occasionally, a storage unit will have lots of trash, broken furniture with no value, and outdated TVs or other appliances. If you can't recycle it or donate it you must take it to the dump or trash container if you have one. I have a very large dumpster like the ones behind most businesses, this costs $95.00 per month for a pick up once per week. I can even put furniture in this container if it fits or if I break it up. People want to get in my dumpster to root around but there is broken glass and rotten food in there so I monitor this closely and refuse to let anyone get in it. The dump nearest my location charges $55.00 per ton. If you have a large amount of trash this is the most economical way to dispose of it. There are cities and towns that have free dump areas so be sure to check the cost at the dump you will be using. If I drive the trash farther out of the city the price is less but the cost of time and gas is higher so I use the local dump. Tires are usually not allowed at the dump or in the dumpster. I pay $2.50 each to dispose of tires, minus the aluminum rims, of course. **KEY:** If the storage facility has a dumpster don't abuse the privilege if they allow you to use it. Storage facility managers will remember how you treated their generosity.

Most storage facilities have a sign reminding customers that they cannot store chemicals, paint, gasoline, and other hazardous items in their storage unit, but small and sometimes large amounts of these items do end up in storage anyway. My city has a program for residential hazardous waste disposal that will accept small amounts of these items. Check your city to see if one exists but remember they only take small amounts. If you discover a large container or containers of unknown chemicals you can usually refuse to take it and the storage facility has to dispose of it. It's better if you don't bid on a unit with large barrels of chemicals unless you know what you are doing.

One of the regular buyers I know bought a unit like this for $1.00. After he looked at it he contacted me to empty it and paid me $400.00 to take the contents, mostly expired vitamin pills 10,000 per bag. I made a trip to the dump and was glad that they considered two tons of vitamin pills ok to throw away. Maybe the soil is richer somewhere because of these vitamins. There was a nice pallet jack in the unit and a few other useful things so I made an adequate profit on it.

Questionable Items:

Pornography to me is degrading to both men and women. I throw away any pornographic DVDs, movies, magazines, and photos that I find either heterosexual or homosexual in nature. I also dispose of any sexually deviant apparatuses that I find in storage units.

Drugs and alcohol are two more questionable items you find in storage units. Alcohol can be disposed of in the safest way possible, especially if opened. Full sealed bottles of wine or alcohol can be given to friends as gifts, if they drink, but use good judgment in doing so. My now deceased husband was an alcoholic so it angered me if someone gave him a bottle of alcohol as a gift. One storage buyer I know donates any liquor he finds to his local VFW meeting place.

Drug paraphernalia, such as pipes, baggies, hypodermic needles, etc. can be found in many storage units. Once these items are spotted in a unit, you need to take extra precautions when cleaning the unit out so you are not cut or punctured with glass or needles. If you do discover a large amount of illicit drugs in a storage unit, notify your local law enforcement agency immediately. I have a huge clear container in my office full of drug paraphernalia that I use when I speak with teens and young adults about the risk of drug abuse, my son-in-law calls it the "loser-fest jar."

Firearms can also be found in storage. I do not handle or sell firearms and the state of California as well as other states have a whole set of regulations for them. If you want to keep a firearm you found in storage it is best to have it run through a licensed gun dealer to determine if it has been reported stolen or lost. Many regular storage unit buyers do this and know all the statutes that regulate firearm sales and/or ownership. The best thing to do is be familiar with your state and local firearm statutes if you plan to keep or sell firearms you have found in a storage unit.

Firearm sales are illegal at swap meets in southern California. Recently a storage buyer carried a shotgun to a swap meet. He let a "friend" and potential customer take a look at the shotgun inside his van. The customer pulled the trigger without checking to see if it was loaded. It blew a hole into the van roof. Thankfully no one was seriously hurt, just scratched by falling debris. The seller, of course, was arrested and will have plenty of fines and court costs to pay. This incident happened just before Sept 11th this year when everyone was on high alert!

CHAPTER 6

Sorting to Sell

A word about selling

Buying storage units for profit is easiest if you know how and where to sell your storage unit contents. After selling at the swap meet and thrift store for thirty years and online for ten years, I have a good idea of what sells for how much and where.

Selling at the swap meet is my current sales niche. There are swap meets, flea markets, and antique shows everywhere, some are inside and some are outside depending on the weather. They all have varying days of operation but usually start very early in the morning. The best customers will be there early. Locate a swap meet/antique show in your area through the internet or ask a friend and visit it to get an idea of what is sold there. **KEY:** Go early as soon as they open. In the used merchandise section find the busiest vendor, observe that they are selling assorted fresh merchandise, at low prices directly out of their vehicle.

The busiest vendors will sell out or slow their sales down by 10:30 or 11:00 a.m. and by noon be packed to go home. Many swap meets have a time restraint before you can leave, usually around 1 or 2 p.m., at the Rose Bowl swap meet it is 3 p.m. before you can leave.

Swap meets are labor intensive because you must unpack and set up tables and merchandise, sell, and then repack everything not sold. However, for the amount you spend for the space, swap meets give you the maximum customer exposure. Hundreds, if not thousands of people will walk by your merchandise. Among them will be dealers looking for items to replenish their shop stock, eBay sellers looking for items to list, as well as, moms and dads looking to stretch their family budget.

I am selling two days per week at the swap meet closest to my home. I sell on Tuesdays and Fridays. I sold on the weekends for many years and now prefer to have my weekends free. Many vendors do very well selling on the weekends.

Selling at a thrift store is different than swap meets in many ways. First, the rent is usually higher and you have utilities and parking to consider. Second, you must be able to draw customers to your location. Third, you will need to keep regular hours for opening and closing.

The advantages for a store are that your merchandise can remain on display tables or shelves. You will not be exposed to extremes in weather. Your customers have more time to hunt for their exact need. Many are willing to sign up on a list for a call when the item they need or want comes in. Larger, hard to move items can stay in one place and your electronics can be plugged in and tested. I have had both thrift store and swap meet space at the same time. Swap meets are a great way to draw customers to your store location.

Selling online is distinctive in the following ways: the buyer must depend on your photos and description of the merchandise. Online buyers from sites like craigslist don't always show up for their appointments, and eBay buyers can change their minds. I find that shipping is the hardest part of eBay sales. There are many who make a great living with online sales and the tutorials and "How to" books abound. I sell online with the user name sharonsthriftstore and bob8311.

About two or three times per year I hold a garage/yard sale. Usually it's when I need to pay an extra bill and have lots of merchandise. My location is good for a garage/yard sale. I plan ahead with a couple of ads, some extra help, and six to eight signs. You can usually get rid of a lot of your extra inventory if you price it low enough. However, I have nothing for sale less than 50 cents. Everyone has 50 cents and you will get a bargain only if you group things together and spend more than $2.00. This is how I sell more and package items at my garage/yard sales. Here are some answers you can give if they ask for a lower price, "No thanks, that's a fair price," or "No thanks, I have a small store or swap meet space and I'll sell it there." Don't be afraid to say "No" if you have nice things and have priced them fairly. Have some cards printed up for your store/swap meet space and direct customers there, too. You can tell people that you buy storage units and they can call you in the future to ask for a certain item.

I sell with a combination of swap meet, craigslist, eBay, half.com, and Amazon, as well as, garage sales and estate sales at my own home. Since storage units provide such a wide assortment of merchandise categories you will find out on your own what sells best and where it sells. I have some categories listed and a brief version of my personal experience selling these goods. **KEY:** A word about dealers is that they always have the money when they make an offer so, make them your best customers. I think it is better to sell an item to a dealer than carry it back and forth trying to get top dollar and risking theft or breakage. Keep a fresh contact list and use it often. Use business cards with a plain back, and so you can help contacts remember you, write on the back of the card what you sold to them or said you could probably find for them.

Alphabetical Listing from Art to Video Games

ART: Paintings, posters, fine art, or children's art is an area most of us need an expert for. You can look up on the internet anything with a signature on it. Prints are usually worth less than original art. Any good magnifying glass can show a close up of a picture and if small dots appear it is a print. If you're not sure and think you may have a masterpiece, show it to a buyer/dealer or two for an opinion, be sure to say it is "not for sale" until you check it out.

Extremely valuable art does not usually make it into a storage unit but it is possible. My most valuable piece of art was a 16x20 oil painting that was signed. I listed it on eBay for $2,500 and sold it to a dealer on eBay for $1,200.

ANTIQUES: A true antique is over 100 years old according to the dictionary. Many items people call antique are vintage or collectable. Vintage 1950s is the correct term for an older round screen TV from 1950. A collectable can be any items of interest to any one person or group of people. People collect stamps, toys, military items, animals, papers, historical items, comics/ and so much more. I have a small collection of hinged ceramic boxes from my buying of storage units. If you find a collection of comics for instance, your best buyer will be a dealer who can find assorted people to buy parts of the collection. A collector usually has many of the comics and needs to fill spaces in his collection. I sold a large collection of owl statues, pins, and necklaces to one person for $75.00. Note that vintage clothing sells well if it is from 1970 or before. Vintage 1950s and before has extra high value, if in good and clean condition.

BABY ITEMS: Baby toys and small furniture items sell well only if they are almost new and very clean. Stuffed animals do not sell well. The only valuable baby item I sold was a sterling silver rattle and picture frame for $50.

BOOKS: A huge amount of books will come your way if you buy storage units. Most are worth $1.00 or $2.00 or less. If you find a book dealer who will buy on a select basis, be sure to accept his fair offer. Amazon and half.com list books by title or ISBN so you can see the price variation. Invest in a smart phone with a bar code reader application or scanner, this way you can check a book anywhere by its ISBN number. To sell books in bulk list them by the box on craigslist, you may only get $3.00 per box but books are heavy and hard to move.

I have over 700 books listed on half.com and must keep a space to store them before they sell. I once found two cases of new books with the same title and sold each book for around $10.00 as soon as they were listed. My favorite book seller/buyer in the L.A. area is Dan at www.iliadbooks.com.

BUSINESS/INDUSTRIAL: Racks, showcases, shelving, restaurant equipment, and office furniture are harder to sell. Locate and ask wholesale sellers of such equipment if they would be interested in knowing about your inventory (if any) of such items. Craigslist, the Penny Saver, and eBay "pick up only" are the best ways to sell such items. **KEY:** Mannequins usually sell well.

My biggest sale on business equipment was an entire "Curves" exercise studio I paid $50 for. I packed it in a big crate and shipped it from California to Idaho. I sold it for $800.00 on eBay but spent hours packing it and had to pay $100.00 for the crate. Unless you have manpower and space avoid storage units with business equipment, especially avoid office desk and chairs. These storage units will sell for a low price at auction because of the work involved; don't be tempted to buy them unless you are pretty sure you can sell them.

CAMERAS AND PHOTO: The best way to research the price of a camera or piece of photo equipment is on eBay. **KEY:** Always be sure to look at completed sales on eBay. Just because an item is listed for $600.00 doesn't mean it will sell for that. Many lenses are very valuable and you can search by highest price to find the names of expensive cameras and lenses. I sell my cameras and photo equipment to a local pawn shop employee.

CELLPHONES AND PDAS: Usually a cell phone or pda found in storage is the older model and may or may not work. Radio Shack and others take old phones in trade during certain promotions. If it's a better quality phone it still has a value of $20.00 to $50.00, even up to $100.00 or more for a used iphone. My eighty-six-year-old friend Rose breaks a cheap phone about once per month so I keep the inexpensive ones for her.

Cell phone chargers and other electronic chargers are plentiful in storage, although they may not be in the same place as the device. They usually will sell for two dollars each. If you have the time, separate them into small zip lock bags with the plug showing so people can try them in their device. Mark the voltage on the bag with a white sticker so customers do not have to open each bag to see it.

CLOTHING, SHOES, AND ACCESSORIES: This category is huge and there is lots to know. Better name brand clothing, shoes, and accessories always have good value. Again, do research on eBay. Regular clothing sells better in a store and in cool weather. Clothing also sells better when hung up or folded on a table. There is a lot of competition on clothing sales from garage sales, swap meets, and second hand stores.

Shoes can bring $50.00 to $100.00 or more if you know your brands well and they are clean and barely worn or new. Belts, neckties, scarves, gloves, and purses all have value also and sell if they are displayed well. Socks and underwear should be donated if clean or tossed if dirty and only sold if new and in the package. Don't feel sorry for clothing that is dirty or ripped, just toss it, no one will buy it and it will make your other clothing look suspect.

Vintage clothing from 1990 or older increases in value the older it gets. Consignment shops can be a great place to sell any clothing. Call or visit them first and ask about their requirements. Consignment stores keep 40 percent or more of the sale price and usually only want to keep the items for thirty to sixty days, then you must pick them up.

Again, explore every angle for selling clothing, because one-fourth of most household storage units consist of clothing. Women's clothing sells better then men's, if you sell from the same rack or display be sure to change your stock on a regular basis. Donate what you cannot sell to local shelters, missions, and the big charities to make room for new stock.

COINS AND PAPER MONEY: Good old or new U.S. currency should go into your bank account. You may find genuine silver coins or foreign coins which have more value as silver. Many coin dealers are very reputable and have a price they pay to you and a price they sell the same coin for. Of course the internet is your best source for research today so go online. Foreign coins may have silver content or be just brass so you want to determine this and it will increase the value if silver. Finding money in storage is not unusual but it is mostly pennies or other small change.

Ten years ago I was at a storage facility that was an older beat up place on a short local street. All the doors at the facility were gray aging wooden ones that swung open on hinges. A unit came up for sale that was about 10x10, piled high with assorted rubbish, clothing, books, and papers, but not a dollar in sight. An old purse and an umbrella with a raincoat hung near the doorway on the wall. The lady manager of the storage facility jokingly said, "The guy who lost this unit must have money in here, he would spend a half hour or more in here before he would come and pay his rent." I bid $25.00 and all the other bidders walked away, mumbling I should have just bid $5.00 and I would have gotten it. I also bought the same owner's second unit that was smaller and had less junk for $5.00.

After paying for my unit I went back to take a quick look and assess the room before I went to get my large truck and some help. I opened the door and saw it was worse than I remembered. I grabbed the purse on the wall and was immediately surprised to see that the only thing in the purse was about $150.00 in paper money! I took it and bought lunch for my helpers and me before we tackled the mess. I brought back three helpers, supplies, and an empty truck. We spent four hours packing, sorting, and gathering a truck full of trash, plus random cash in the form of loose change, $1.00, $5.00, and $10.00 bills. All total there was $1,680.00 in cash of which $400.00 was in loose change. Speculating on where the previous owner got all this money, I assumed he was a homeless scrapper who is someone who gathers scrap metal: cans, bottles, and cashes them in. His small cash hoard along with his accumulated trash obviously had value to him. I could further speculate that he may be in custody and unable to pay his rent, which happens frequently to homeless individuals.

COLLECTIBLES: As I mentioned earlier in this chapter, a collectable can be any item of interest to any one person or group of people. Collections can be empty or full beer cans each one different, license plates, animals, postcards, comics (which I covered extensively earlier), trains, or toys; basically any item collected as a hobby. Items are collected for display as an investment in hopes of future appreciation or just for enjoyment or fun. Finding a collection in a storage unit means you will need to find the other person who may be interested in this collection; I will send you again to eBay or craigslist.

After almost thirty years in the second hand business I cannot begin to tell you what people will collect and who is interested in it. My biggest personal collection from all my storage units I have bought is old and expired driver's licenses, I have no idea why I collected them and they have little value, but that's my collection.

COMPUTERS AND COMPONENTS: Personal computers, towers, and printers abound in storage but most are obsolete by the time the storage unit comes for sale. However, you can find high end laptops, monitors, servers, and peripheral items occasionally. Many computer parts are not commonly recognizable and you need to develop a friendship with a technical computer person. Again, I cannot stress this enough, dealers are your friends, they can make money from your stuff if you cultivate a friendship by allowing them to buy from you and they will be more willing to evaluate things for you. **KEY:** Most apple products hold their value well.

In Los Angeles computer scrap has value. Old computer towers can be sold for $.03 per pound including the case. The sound cards that have gold pins can be sold for $3.00 per pound as of this writing. Investigate selling computer scrap in your nearest big city or online. It may pay better than you realize and is worth investigating. Certain used printer ink cartridges can be exchanged for paper at office supply stores. Many schools or organizations have recycling programs that you can donate to.

CRAFTS: Craft items sell well if you have the patience to sort them and/or group the items. Many teachers, as well as, individuals work with craft projects and keeping your price affordable will help to sell items some storage unit buyers throw away. Art supplies sell best followed by needle crafts and stamping supplies. Find the parent-teacher coordinator for your local elementary school, they usually have a budget for craft supplies and are delighted to have that budget go a little bit further.

My best craft find was at a friend's thrift store where they were busily dumping small stickers, decorative paper, tiny craft items, and more into the dumpster. I halted the process and took all the rest and still have craft items two years later that come in handy when children are around.

DOLLS AND BEARS: Very good condition antique and collectable dolls have value. Even the dolls or bears in rough condition but are vintage have some value. The newer made dolls, unless it's Barbie, are quite low in value. Barbies have their own category of collectors and still sell to the public for a nice price. Dolls that are "played with," have cut hair or markers used all over their face or body, have little or no value. Bears have their own category heading on eBay. Rare means value, even in distressed condition, look them up especially if they have a tag, or metal button in the ear.

Just this week I bought a storage unit with more than fifteen large boxes of assorted dolls and toys in varying condition. The only money I will make, other than the dollar each for the rest, is on the new unopened Barbies that were in the assortment. **KEY:** NIB on eBay means New in Box.

DVDS AND MOVIES: At most swap meets you can buy used DVDs for $3.00 or two for $5.00. To sell DVDs online they must be in really great condition or you risk a returned item. Always give a true description and let the buyer be pleased with the arrival of their DVD in "better than described" condition. VHS tapes have little value unless they are a rare film that hasn't been transferred to DVD.

Film is something that doesn't appear very often in storage. Small old cartoons or travel films are of interest to collectors. Some film is collectable, open a reel and look five to ten feet down the reel many times you will be able to find an interesting title. My friend Ed recently bought a room full of old film and film cans. He has not been able to sell much of it and may end up donating it to one of the local film schools for a tax deduction. Film Preservation Association's David Shepard is interested in any vintage black and white film and owns the Black Hawk Films, film collection.

EBAY MOTORS: eBay has a whole separate site for auto parts, accessories, and whole cars. Most auto parts found in storage units are scrap metal, some people save their old brake pads, mufflers, or chrome trim for some reason. However, new auto part items, like seat covers, lights, and identifiable body parts have greater value.

My friend Bill who's an eBay seller by the name of auction-buys-2009 is great at identifying auto parts. Recently I picked up his leftovers from an auto parts storage unit. He had sold a motor out of it and made a great profit then left the rest for me. He identified a 2007 Ford Mustang hood and seats for me in the same unit, which I sold for $400.00 because I was able to exactly identify those items. The rest of the items from that unit were scrap metal or trash.

Whole cars are not commonly found inside storage units but at on-site parking areas located on storage facilities, they do come up for auction occasionally. These cars have usually been parked for a long period of time and will result in extra expenses to prepare them for sale. You may even end up having to pay for towing to move them off the storage facility property. They must also go through a lien sale process in California before they can be sold if they were hidden inside the unit.

ENTERTAINMENT MEMORABILIA AND AUTOGRAPHS: Since Los Angeles is where I live, I am more likely to find entertainment memorabilia. Autographs have their own special category because collectors may want signatures, letters, or other signed items from famous or infamous people.

It pays to search paperwork in any storage unit, even if it is not in the name of a famous person. Very recently, someone purchased a storage unit that was in the name of an accounting firm who was, it turned out, the firm paying a very famous female's bills. The firm had changed addresses and neglected to notify the storage facility, this caused the person's storage unit to be sold at auction. The buyer of the unit was looking through the paperwork and realized the unit belonged to someone very famous. Not only was there paperwork and contracts but personal items of clothing, jewelry, and tapes. The buyer of this storage unit sold some items on eBay, then all of the remaining items back to the owner, for an huge and undisclosed amount of money.

GIFT CARDS AND COUPONS: Many storage units that have personal items will have gift cards or certificates. Currently I believe I have an unused gift card in an old purse from a storage unit. I know for sure I have a manicure certificate for $25.00; I just haven't been able to get to that manicure salon to use it. I was actually very surprised to see more than 3,000 listings on eBay for gift cards. I don't understand why someone would pay $24.03 for a $25.00 Starbucks card? While searching the same site I saw a $300.00 Starbucks card listed for $75.00 with fourteen hours to go. I bid $95.00 and it surprised me that by the time the bidding closed it sold for $295.00. **KEY:** Gift cards sell very well.

HEALTH AND BEAUTY: Storing health products, vitamins, and first aid is common. Make up, nail polish, and hair products are also found in storage. Most products are opened and used or expired so just discard them. Sealed fragrances, both perfume and men's cologne, are easy to sell. Medical supplies such as braces and wheelchairs can be sold, while crutches and older style walkers are good for aluminum scrap.

HOME AND GARDEN: A household storage unit will have decorative items, such as, vases, knick knacks, baskets, throw rugs, and furniture. Quality modern or vintage furniture sells best in good condition but for a fraction of their new value. Preserve the value of great furniture by using blankets, pads, or even cardboard to protect it while packing. Never put metal shelves or racks next to or touching wood, even the smallest jiggle will scratch the wood. If the furniture has to be disassembled to move it, be careful to package screws, nuts, and other brackets together with the furniture by taping them inside. Selling furniture at a swap meet is tough because people come to swap meets, not expecting to transport big items home. Dealers are the fastest way to sell furniture. For furniture sales there are also auction houses that are constantly in need of new stock. You may have to wait until after their next auction before you get paid for your item, sometimes your item doesn't sell and you have to wait even longer to get paid.

Craigslist is a great selling place for furniture. The main drawback is that you must have a place to display it. Be honest when they ask about where you got the furniture and sell it fast if you get a decent offer. Moving furniture around is damaging to legs, as well as burdensome to you and your help.

Appliances usually work when they are found in storage units. Stoves, refrigerators, washer & dryers and small appliances sell better with a guarantee. Refrigerators that have been stored with the door closed will most likely have mold. If any food was stored there you will have problems removing the bad food smell. If the refrigerator is really nice, modern, and works (check before you clean), cleaning it up will increase its value by 40 percent or more.

The home and garden category is where most items found is storage belong. There are too many items to mention, such as, tools, garden and outdoor living items, holiday and party supplies, lamps, carpets, and window accessories, just to name a few. To see more and to answer questions about how to sell these items go to; www.secretsinstorage.com where I will post questions and answers. .

JEWELRY AND WATCHES: Costume jewelry is my favorite to sell. Women and sometimes men will adorn themselves with jewelry before buying clothing or anything else. Accessories such as earrings and rings enhance a woman's appearance. Costume jewelry abounds in storage. Costume jewelry that has a name on it has more value. Names like Monet,

Liz Taylor, Miriam Haskell, and Vogue can all be looked up on eBay.

Most jewelry boxes have something that glitters and sparkles in them and all of it is very easy to sell, among the costume jewelry there is often pieces of silver and gold. Today's sky high gold prices and increasing silver prices mean that one piece of gold that weighs twenty grams at $25.00 per gram will bring $500.00. To figure the approximate price of gold scrap you can use this formula; (today's gold price) times .585 for 14K gold times .92 equals the price per ounce you should expect. To get a price per gram, divide the final number by 31.5.

Here is an example; as of 10/24/2011 at www.goldprice.com the price of gold was $1655.00 this times .585 = $968.00 this times .92 = $890.00 price per ounce 14K gold, divide $890.00 by 31.5 = $28.27 which is the price per gram for 14K gold. Gold that is 10K will be less per ounce and 18K will be more. Today, places buying gold are everywhere, even at the swap meet. For your convenience in the appendix you will find the formula for precious scrap metal. By selling at the price using this formula from the appendix the buyer will still be able to make a profit and so will you.

Men love watches, although that is changing with the younger generations. They all have cell phones they use to tell the time with now. Wind up watches always have more value than a quartz or battery operated watch. When I get a large group of watches together I pull out the wind up watches for their higher value. Then I take the other watches and try to find a place that will put in watch batteries for a dollar each. Recently, I found online, assorted common watch batteries in packs of 100 for $5.00. Putting watch batteries in takes patience and time. You need a special place to do it, too because the parts are small and easily lost.

MUSIC: This includes CDs, records, and cassette tapes, most household storage units have some kind of music. CDs have resale value if the CD is inside the jewel case and the paperwork is present. It is pretty easy to list them on half.com, Amazon.com, or other music resale sites. Records or "vinyl" as they are called are collectable and sales depend on condition, both of the record and the cover. Some storage rooms have multiplies of the same record or CD, these are harder if not impossible to sell. Records cannot be recycled but I have found a pastor who will buy the multiple CDs for the jewel case. Cassette tapes have minimal value and I usually just throw them away, especially if they are home recordings.

Once I found 200 boxes of CDs in storage from three or four different artists. One artist I had never heard of. I looked him up on the internet and his CDs were valued at over $10.00 each. I sold all 400 CDs, ten boxes, for $3000 to a CD resale dealer. The remaining thirty boxes went to the pastor to reuse. It pays to look up a name in situations like this. Usually loose CDs, records, and tapes are scratched or damaged, have little value and end up in the trash.

MUSICAL INSTRUMENTS: I don't know anyone who is an expert on all types of musical instruments. Again, name brands and condition are the best indicators for determining value. Some new guitars are just $25.00 while certain name brand guitars even used may be worth thousands. Musical instruments of any type are very easy to sell. You can't always see musical instruments in a storage unit. When you see a guitar case or two that doesn't mean the instrument is inside. Storage units with musical stuff showing will always bring higher bids. Some storage unit buyers research the names of former owners if published to see if any were musicians.

PET SUPPLIES: Storage units contain few pet items; you might find an occasional leash, dog coat or bowl and even sometimes a nice bird cage. My biggest find for animal/pet supplies was eighteen cases of mane and tail shampoo. My thrift store location borders on horse country so we sold it fast by the case.

POTTERY AND GLASS: Selling breakable items at a swap meet means packing with newspaper or other packing material then repacking with like material before you leave. Each time you handle glass or pottery there are dangers of chips or breakage. Sell it fast at bargain prices. Of course, there are exceptions and if you browse a couple of antique shops and eBay you can recognize better pieces. Baccarat crystal glass goblets valued at $120.00 each were thrown in the trash last week because each one had a large chip on the base that could not be repaired.

SPORTING GOODS: This category is huge. From baseballs and bats, volleyballs, and nets, a lot of sporting goods can be found in storage. Use it, sell it, or list it; most items will sell well. One storage unit I acquired contained over 300 new, undrilled bowling balls. There was some scrap metal and a large easy to sell industrial style tool (possibly a drill) in the same unit with the bowling balls so I was sure to make money. The balls were packed in boxes of four with a total weight of sixty-four pounds per box. Since I own a large empty lot I stacked them on pallets and covered them, excited to start selling. Then . . . nothing! Oh, I sold a few for $15.00 each and I tried to call bowling alleys but three years later, after the boxes had disintegrated I decided to hopefully be able to give them away. At least I would not have to take them to the dump. I put an ad on craigslist for over 280 free bowling balls. Four different guys came the same day and picked up 110, 80, 50, and the remainder. At least I didn't have to throw over two tons of solid inert waste into the landfill. What the guys would do with so many bowling balls I have no idea! **KEY:** If you find no buyer for something in your storage unit and none of your charity friends want it, place a free ad on craigslist. The results will surprise you.

SPORTS MEMORABILIA: In the sports card category alone there are over four million listings on eBay. Look it up, there is no other quick way to find the value of sports card except to go to completed sales on eBay. Baseball cards are usually more collectable than other sports cards, and before 1980 is better. There are also two million listings for sports fan apparel and souvenirs on eBay so be sure to look that up also. If you think it is collectable in this category sell it as such.

Recently, a storage unit buyer that I know came across an extensive collection of vintage boxing related items. Another buyer offered to help him sell it and asked him not to throw anything away. The first buyer who owned the collection had his wife help him package up the contents. She threw away a ratty, dirty, silk robe from one of the most famous boxers ever. It was worth well over $10,000.00 and caused a pretty big family rift. **KEY:** Be careful that your helpers, if you use help, know what they are doing and can follow instructions well.

STAMPS: Unless stamps are found in a stamp collector book, I assume they have only face value. It's a wonder the U.S. Post office isn't well off financially as a result of all the unused postage stamps that I find in storage. Stamps found in storage units over the years mean that I will never have to buy stamps. I have hundreds of stamps in all denominations. Recently, I found $30.00 worth of fifty-two cent stamps, good for shipping small books.

The post office will give you other stamps for stamps that are stuck together but you have to ask them how they want you to bring them in. My post office asks that they be unstuck any way you can without damaging the face, and then glued carefully onto a plain sheet of paper in neat order so that they can count them fast.

TOYS AND HOBBIES: Finding toys in storage is great! My family tries out new toys, old toys, and board games which abound in household storage units. Puzzles usually are thrown out unless sealed. Models are very popular and older models that are new in the box bring good money. Again, there are millions of items in assorted categories in the toys and hobbies section of eBay. The search function allows you to be very specific for what you are trying to research.

Some inventors with ideas pay to have thousands of their toys or models manufactured and then find out the market is not very good for their item. One storage unit that I picked up had over 2,500 assorted boxes of miniature brick construction sets. About twenty-five different boxed mini-block sets for assorted age groups were included. I know why they ended up in storage; they were very heavy for shipping; one to ten pounds and very difficult to assemble. I donated over 1,000 to Job Core in downtown L.A., sold a few, and still have hundreds taking up space in my storage unit.

VIDEO GAMES: Xbox, Wii, and playstation games and consoles all sell well. Important when finding these games is to keep the boxes, cases, cords, controls, and paperwork together. Test it out in order to sell them with the statement "it works."

This alphabetical list only begins to cover the myriad of items that you will find in storage units. Dust and dirt are plentiful but remember someone thought it valuable enough to pay for storing it, so maybe it does have value to someone else.

CHAPTER 7

Stories from Storage

Some Stories

TWO STORIES ABOUT SOME SAFES: I have seen many safes in storage. One buyer I know will buy any unit with a safe, but from personal experience and knowledge I would say that 90 percent of safes in storage are empty. However, there is the 10 percent that surprise you. The following are two stories of mine about safes.

Hector, who is another storage buyer, knows that I have a big truck and will pick up leftovers. Hector called me to pick up a storage unit he bought but didn't want. He said, "There is a safe in there and an old motorcycle." After assuring him I would get the unit, he gave me the key and said, "It's kind of messy." The room was on the third floor of an old moving and storage building that had a huge freight elevator that forty people could stand in. The elevator had the bulky doors that had to be closed and push buttons that had to be held down to keep the elevator moving. Painted red streaks on each floor and streaks in the elevator labeled where you must stop so you would be level with the floor. Once we found the room and opened the doors, one at each end, this large 10x20 foot unit had a large safe we could see. It was behind several beat up useless dressers, chests, and shelves that were piled with clothing shoes and paperwork. We worked to remove the clutter around the safe. The clothing and shoes were all men's wear and all vintage 1960s & '70s. After we managed to get half of the unit loaded we uncovered another smaller safe and not one but two small motorcycles. It turned out to be a full truck load and I was excited about the safes. The guy didn't spend money on clothing or furniture so he must have everything in the safe right, or so I assumed?

As it turned out, the '60s and '70s clothing and shoes were worth over $200.00. The motorcycles brought in $250.00 and since I had a thrift store at this time the furniture was saleable after all. I called a friend, Jack from my church, who owns a lock and safe company. He came after work and drilled out both safes, being careful on the larger safe that he said he would take on consignment. The larger safe held ten or twelve Eisenhower dollar coins and one silver dollar from 1928 and a Zippo lighter. The smaller safe was empty. Jack eventually sold the safe for $300.00, half of which was mine. I didn't buy the unit myself, so I did well after accounting for labor and truck expenses.

My second story began with a call from a moving and storage company that holds auctions. They had two large safes and

wanted me to pick them up. They have a great loading dock so I took my truck, my son Marco and we picked up two jumbo bulky matching safes. They had round metal wheels that only moved side to side, we loaded them in the truck and tied them down. I didn't have the thrift store yet, but I had a large empty lot where I could drop them off. I needed an empty truck for the next day. I stopped at the lot, opened the gate and backed in. I assumed these safes were probably empty, they were still locked so we pushed them off the truck. We heard a thud inside and figured it was maybe a shelving unit. We were curious now so my son Marco went home to get his grinder. Sparks flew as he worked for over an hour and used three new blades on his grinder, to be a "safe cracker."

We destroyed the door of the first safe and we were eventually ready to lift off what was left of it. What we found makes me cringe at the thought of all the cutting and drilling we did. The safe was packed full of ammunition. There were shot gun shells both 12 and 20 gauge, 22 cartridges, 38 & 9 mm shells, all new in full boxes. Over 200 pounds of ammunition, enough for a small army! Now the logical thought was that the other matching safe must contain the guns but we didn't want to destroy it and it was too dark to work anymore. We packed the ammo into the truck to take home and the next day I called Jack the safe guy again. He couldn't come out to see the safe so we loaded it and took it to his shop and waited. Two days later we found out the second safe was EMPTY! I gave the ammunition to a trusted friend who has his own shooting range for a $900.00 donation to our church's youth camp. My friend

trains young men in gun safety and shooting. Jack sold the safe that was empty and I made $100.00. The real story behind this safe story is that if I had opened the empty safe first, I probably would have loaded both and pushed them off at the scrap metal yard. The explosion that may have happened if they were both crushed by the bulldozer, is still in my mind. I don't know if ammo explodes, but who wants to take that chance?

THE STORY OF UNIT C58: This was a small unit and there was only one wicker clothing hamper inside. I figured no one else would bid for it because laundry hampers usually contain dirty laundry. I bid $1.00 and won. I didn't put a lock on the unit because I went back upstairs for my winnings soon after I paid for them.

From the contents of the hamper I could tell the tenant was female. A Roca Wear size 3x denim jacket was on top of the contents. It was in really good condition so I thought that my dollar investment would get a nice return. I ended up giving it away to an extra large friend when cold weather arrived. Among the other things was a folded up traffic ticket, for riding on public transportation without paying the fare. Usually the fine for this is over $100, so our C58 gal may be in police custody if she failed to appear in traffic court.

Most units have trash and trash talks! Her trash said that this gal used public transportation, ate cheap, and was either black or had curly hair. I have found many condoms in units, this one had a few. There was a girl's generic designer clutch purse, a half

smoked cigar and another small zipper bag with a variety of business cards, i.e. a nail salon, phone store, and a car lot, etc.

THE STORY OF UNIT 3154: This unit was upstairs and almost empty for its size, a refrigerator, and six large boxes were the only items inside. The boxes looked like someone had already opened them and the top one was obviously empty. I got the room for a bid of $30.00. I knew the refrigerator would bring me a profit if it worked and they usually do.

It turned out that the boxes were not empty, there were lots of children's DVDs and some nice clothing. The lady clamored to the office that she wanted her computer back. It was an older tower style computer of little value. I left the computer and personal photos, school pictures of her kids, and some letters at the office.

And, this lady had a whip, no other sex paraphernalia just a whip.

She also had a box full of worn shoes and slippers with no mates; why? I threw these away. I found a box of new children's toys, which I took home. I have a chest at home with items that I keep for birthdays, special visits by children and other occasions, these items would help to replenish it.

THE STORY OF UNIT A155: I paid $200.00 for this unit, it was clean and neat, plus it was downstairs. I could see a clean iron baker's rack, clean mattress, some stools, neatly packed boxes, along with a small tool box. When I started to sort through things, these two flashlights were one of the first things I found.

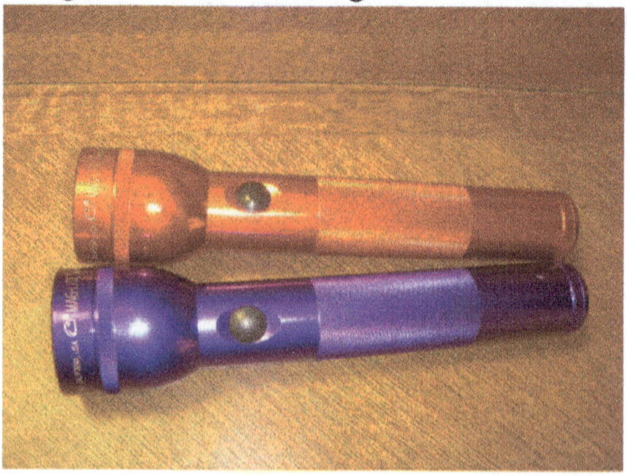

They even had batteries that were not worn down completely and I took them home. I also took home a thermos, a pocket knife, and some crazy glue. New toy trucks in their original boxes were in this unit and they were easy items to sell. There were nice clean household items; a microwave, dishes, pots and pans, silverware, and some good small kitchen appliances.

This guy worked as a cashier at a food service place and some fast food places. I knew this because of the name on the aprons I found. He still couldn't make enough money because he had these notices in his stuff. One is a shut off from the Department of Water and Power, the other is three-day pay or quit notice from his landlord and then he lost his storage.

This was probably the previous owner's most prize possession, a nice collection of Zippo lighters. I used this picture for eBay and sold the collection for $350.00.

THE STORY OF UNIT 3037: This is a disgusting story, beware if you are easily offended. This unit was on the third floor, 5x10 feet in size and a notice was given at the beginning of the auction that the owner of the unit was downstairs and wanted his (antibiotics) prescription medication back from inside the unit. The unit was a trashy mess, piled over eighteen inches deep on the floor and only the hanging coats looked decent. No one else was bidding so I bid $1.00 and won. I put on my lock and went to the rest of the rooms at auction that day.

When I came back later with my son and grandson to empty this unit, we bagged up all the clothing, separated the trash, and

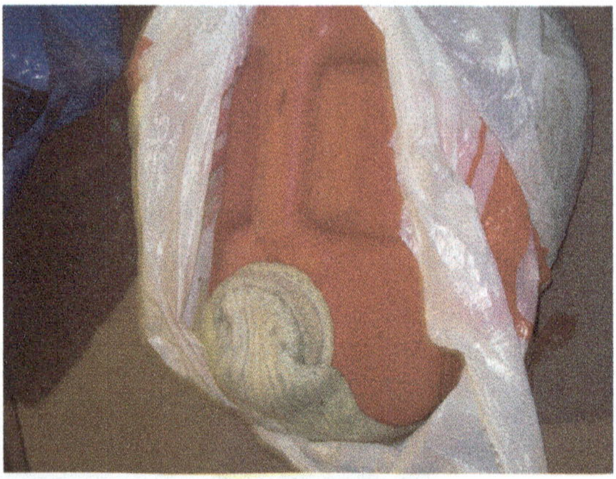

found a two-gallon red gas can in a plastic bag. It was obviously full and after un-wrapping the bag, found that a sock had been placed over the opening. It was wet from the movement and instead of the smell of gas, we were gagging from the smell of urine. Since this unit was on the third floor, the owner probably found it easier to use this can instead of traveling downstairs to the bathroom.

There were some new items in this unit, obsolete cell phone covers, a pile of baseball caps, and knitted caps. These caps were easy to sell and about the only thing of real value in the unit. I returned the only medication that I found; a huge group of testosterone patches. I also returned his family pictures that he didn't even ask about.

THE STORY OF UNIT 152: My friend Sam gave me this unit because he had already looked and didn't want to load the mattress. I guess he only paid a dollar and left the "good stuff" for me. From the door you could see a mattress, a flower vase and well… not much else. I help Sam because he leaves me stuff in units that I can make money on.

There was a trophy from a small town in northern California, the crown was attached to a threadbare pillow. This girl who won a trophy may have had some talent and left her happy family behind in the small town to compete here in L.A., then

she lost her storage. There was a Gorilla amplifier, not worth much, but it told me that maybe this girl was a singer and/or played the guitar. I didn't keep her name from the trophy to look her up on the internet so I will never know if she made it in the big city.

THE STORY OF UNIT 68: When they opened the door on this unit, everyone (except me) stepped back. Maybe the wind wasn't blowing my way but I couldn't smell the cat odor. I bid $20.00 and no one bid or said anything so I put on my lock. I knew there was some trash, so when we came back we were prepared for it, but… the smell was overwhelming. The lady had more cats than Animal Regulations allowed. I know this because there was a citation from Animal Regulations warning her about the allowable number of cats and also a list of the chemicals that she could purchase to eliminate odor. Pictures of the lady, who was blonde, middle-aged, and appeared friendly, were in the unit.

There was a nice small oval cabinet with a drawer, cute for any home décor but upon opening the door, well… take a look.

The crumbs that you see in the picture are body parts. . . of cockroaches!! Legs, wings, eggs, and poop were in the cabinet. As much as I loved the look and design, sorry, it went to the dump. Cockroaches lay eggs and I think the eggs are like seeds stored in the Pyramids, they come to life even after centuries.

Most of the ceramic, metal, and stone decorative items in this unit could be cleaned. However, this lady moved in a hurry so some unwanted things got left behind. In the two views of the same pan, one view is of the outside and when I saw something moving inside the pan, I just shuddered,

snapped a picture, and wrapped it back up for the dump. Maybe she was evicted and the manager, as required by law, had to promptly store her apartment full of things. It surely looked like that was the case in this unit.

There was a box with two stick horses; a white one and a black one, their battery operated sound long gone. Since we encounter lots of items stored by people who seem to be obsessive/compulsive, this may have been the case for this lady. Along with the stick horses there were bags of new items with the tags still on. Even the clothing was new with the tags still on and not worn. Her wallet was packed full of receipts and over forty-five, one-dollar bills sandwiched between papers. Clothing sells well, but the stench that permeated the clothing would be an issue. We were going to throw it away; however, we placed the items on hangers, hung them on the outside fence at the thrift store and let the fresh air do its work. Many ladies won't resist an item with a new tag on valued between $22.00-$28.00, which we were selling for a dollar or two each; they will even overlook the odor.

I kept a nice decorative water fountain, new with tags priced at $129.00 from a builder's discount store. It stayed outside for a month so I could make sure that there were no bugs or smell. It cost me $65.00 to go to the dump with debris from this unit, about $50.00 in labor cost, and I sold over $300.00 in decorative items plus the cash I found so the profit was slim, but ok. This unit was one of the worst I have ever worked on.

THE STORY OF UNIT 28: Wow! What a mess, but that means it would be pretty cheap. Yes, only $30.00 for this unit and I took two pictures of the inside.

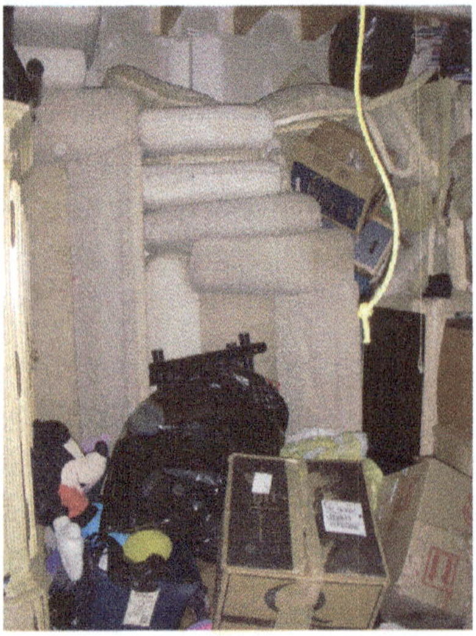

The second one is after I got it halfway empty so you could see the big couches that were a surprise. Most of the time in this type of unit the couches are dirty or torn and so they go to the dump. It took about two hours and three people to empty this unit, there would not be much profit after labor cost.

There were multiple pairs of stepping out shoes which could be sold for not more than a few dollars each. The owner of this unit had three little girls; I knew this from the family photos. The girls had toys and more toys, and each had a current TV cartoon character pink backpack. Over 100 Barbie doll miniatures from Happy Meals I think, each one had a wire twisted around it possibly for a Barbie doll tree at Christmas. A reproduction of a Mohammad Ali boxing jacket; one of my workers saw it and got excited thinking it was real, but it was just another piece of clothing to hang in the thrift store. The owner of this unit was Hispanic and there was a disco ball probably used for parties. It was pretty dusty and missing some colors, too so maybe they let the children play with it. I thought it had value but it wasn't worth much in its condition. All in all my profit from this unit was small.

A STORY FROM MOVING & STORAGE CRATES: I bought two of these crates for $150 at a moving company. I couldn't see much when they opened the crates but knew they had been stored for a long time. If you pay attention you can hear the comments made in conversations between the storage

company owner and the auctioneer. One comment I heard was, "This guy has had this stuff here since the '80s and always paid, he must have died." Lots of old clothing in the crate, not vintage enough to be valuable and some nice vintage home stereo equipment. I was happy with the price. Nothing else stood out in these two containers, just ordinary house wares that were sellable and some couches that had to be thrown away.

This Magnatone lap steel guitar was in the crate, it was pretty beat up. A friend gave me the metal slide for it to make it look more

complete and I had someone check it so I could advertise it as working. I ended up getting $150.00 for it. There was a Luxman turntable that was very heavy, about eighty pounds and it said "belt drive" on the back. I know vintage audio equipment has value. I looked it up on eBay and found that one had sold for more than $400.00, so I listed it on craigslist. Craigslist is easy, has a place for digital pictures, is free and local, so no shipping fee. Someone called right away and paid me $350.00 for it. An RX-202 cassette deck was part of the audio equipment too. I hooked it up and saw that it worked and this one turned the cassette around when it came to the end. Since the turntable had value, I assumed that this would sell well and it did, for $100. All total I made about $400.00 on these crates.

THE STORY OF UNIT 705: I bid $50.00 for this storage unit; it was downstairs which was good since this was a full 10x10 foot unit. From the door you could see some old couches, speakers, and lots of bags of clothing; it appeared to be a man's stuff. The guy who owned this unit spent extra money to buy a disc lock. They are a little bit harder to cut but they cut just the same. The storage company throws these locks inside the unit when they cut them off, just more junk for me to throw away. Sometimes there are two or three cut locks, saying that more than two or three times they have gone past their due date and almost lost their unit.

There was a nice set of intact Mexican maracas in the unit that were an easy sale for $10.00. One plastic bag had the man's first aid/shaving kit, new razors, band-aids, deodorant & batteries, an electric razor, nail clippers, and other assorted sundry items. Ever wonder where your emblem went off your car? Well, this guy had ten that I could see and some more in a bag, maybe he was a collector? In case of emergency there were some jumper cables and a Bible in one box. I also found some nice yellow rope in the

box that I am still using and assorted socks clean and dirty. I find more dirty socks than I ever want to remember. The surprise in this unit was that among the junk and dirty clothes there was a crystal bowl still in the box worth about $60.00.

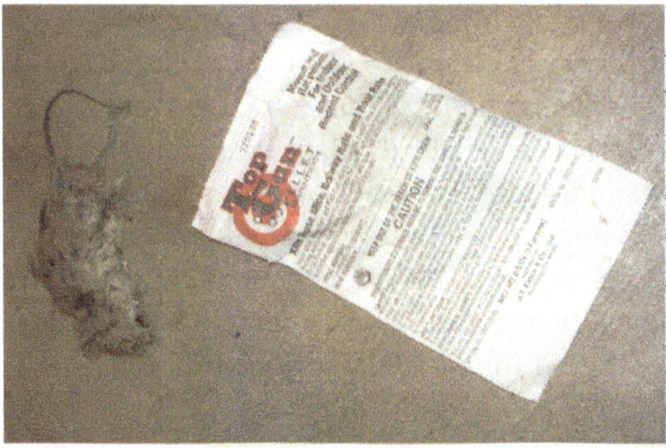

Thankfully, this mouse had been dead for a long time, was all dried up and didn't smell. Almost all storage facilities have some sort of pest control and this one had this "Top Gun" pellet pouch inside which had done its job on the mouse. Since the unit must be completely empty, I took this furry guy and disposed of him. My total profit for this unit was $200.

A PERSONAL STORY: Since I accumulate lots of extra "stuff" as a storage unit buyer I rented a large 10x40 container, the type you see on the back of semi trucks, for my overflow because the price was so good. The container was located in a storage yard on top of a hill about five miles from my home. One winter, my two helpers and I headed up the winding road to the top of the hill and my storage container to get some things for the swap meet, at the time there was a cold twenty to twenty-five mile an hour wind blowing and some light sprinkles. I parked, opened the creaky heavy metal door and we all went inside to gather an assortment of heavy sweat shirts from the boxes stored there. We commented to each other how hard the wind was blowing, when CLANK! A gust of wind blew the heavy container door closed. The three of us laughed those nervous laughs of people in a bad situation that hope things will work out. First, I tried to shove the door with all my might but realized it had actually latched when it slammed shut. There was a whirling metal air turbine that was going around and around faster and faster, so we knew we could breathe and we had a small amount of light. I knew from previous visits to this container on the hill that the cell phone reception was limited and being inside the container made it worse. I decided to try anyway and by standing on some boxes, holding the phone up near the turbine I was relieved that I was able to call my son who lived nearby. I told him our situation and he laughed in disbelief. I gave him the facilities' gate code and the unit number and he arrived fifteen minutes later to rescue us from the container. He entered the container to see if he wanted some of the sweat shirts we were getting, when to his disbelief a gust of wind blew the door shut and latched it again!! He realized then how it happened to us. Fortunately, one of my helpers had gone to my truck to get something when the door slammed shut the second time; she came right away and unlatched and opened the door for us. **KEY:** On a windy day make sure to prop your door open with something pretty heavy.

Most Unique Finds

ED'S STORY: Ed has been a regular storage buyer and friend of mine for twenty-five years. He is willing to pay a formidable price for a storage unit that he likes and that looks good to him. In 1994, almost twenty years ago, Ed bid and won a storage unit about 10x10 located in Northridge, California, northeast of Los Angeles. The unit was packed full of nice household items, great stereo, oriental carpets, and more so he bid up to $2,350.00 and won.

Ed is a buyer who looks at his purchase as he packs it into his van. He likes to leave behind personals on the day of purchase so he doesn't have to return. After packing most of it into his vehicle he was disappointed at the value of the merchandise found. There were a couple of rifles and a handgun that have value but his remaining hope was based on the contents of three large trunks still in the unit. They were covered with car covers and surrounded by what looked like moth crystals.

Ed moved the first trunk into the hallway to have a better look at it and open it. When he moved it he noticed a damp spot where it had been standing. The trunk was wrapped in duct tape, over and over again, then a thick plastic sheet and more duct tape, over a half inch thick. As he cut through the tape a foul odor filled the air. A friend with Ed that day was a retired LAPD, and he stated to Ed and the property manager that it was probably nothing, but Ed had the property manager call the police. Two female officers arrived and also felt that is was probably nothing but spoiled meat in a mini refrigerator. However, they stayed to witness the opening.

As Ed continued to cut the tape the stench became unbearable, many trips outside to gasp for fresh air and a pry bar finally got the trunk open. Yes, the trunk contained a dead body that had liquefied and Ed's unit became a crime scene. The coroner came to remove the remains from the first trunk and took the other two trucks unopened, as well.

There were three bodies total in the unit, two men and one woman. Ed, who had touched everything, had to remove the contents from his van and place the items into a separate company storage unit. The guns were turned over to the police. The hand gun was a .38 revolver and turned out to be the murder weapon. Ed was fingerprinted, cleared, and released.

The two men had been shot and the woman was killed by blunt force trauma. The Indonesian man who placed the bodies in the storage unit was a former business partner of the trio. He had frozen the bodies before he put them in the storage unit, paid one year in advance and then fled to Indonesia. Upon learning of the murders the Indonesian government placed the man under arrest and tried him for the murders. One of the victims was a very prominent Indonesian businessman. After finding the man guilty, the rumor has it that he was shot by a firing squad the next day. As a side note, the check for six months worth of storage for the unit arrived at the storage facility a week after the unit was sold at auction. You can read more about this story by going online at www.google.com and typing into search the words "three dead bodies Northridge storage."

Most Unique Finds:

1. 2,000 small stuffed penguins
2. Sixty-five different sizes and styles of rubber duckies
3. Ingrid's gall stones in a jar
4. A strap on fake pregnancy belly
5. A 4,000 lb part to a crane
6. A cement gargoyle
7. 300 boxes of thank you cards
8. two boxes of asphalt
9. twenty-five men's shirt collars
10. Whiley Boy's ashes in a very nice small chest (a family pet)

Things in Almost Every Storage:

When you buy a storage unit at auction there are some items that you will find in almost every storage, i.e. cardboard, paper, pens, pennies, clothing, unopened mail, and a broken lock.

Personal household storage units make up most of the storage units bought at auction and usually you find a percentage of the following:

45% - have Bibles

85% - have Christmas decorations

80% - have a blender, toaster, and pans

75% - have groceries/food that is expired

60% - have dirty laundry

90% - have suitcases or travel bags

And almost all have evidence of broken lives. "Do not lay up for yourselves treasures on earth, where moth and rust destroy and where thieves break in and steal; but lay up for yourselves treasures in heaven, where neither moth nor rust destroys and where thieves do not break in and steal. For where your treasure is, there your heart will be also." Matthew 6:19-21 (King James Version)

I repeat what I said earlier in this book, you will have to work hard, and you may not always make a profit. It's interesting work and sometimes fun, but not for everyone. Be sure to check the website www.secretsinstorage.com for new and interesting units. Also watch for the documentary that we are making for release in about a year.

Appendix

Auction checklist

Storage Unit Cleanout checklist

Resources

Paperwork Examples

Some Frequently Asked Questions

AUCTION CHECKLIST
PREPARED THE DAY BEFORE AUCTION

Storage Facility Name ____________________
Example; Public Storage

Storage Facility Address ____________________
Example; 7800 Whitsett

Time ____________________
Example; 10:00 a.m.

____

____

____

____

____

____

____

Tools: _____Cash

_____Flashlight

_____Locks & Keys

_____Resale permit (optional)

____

NOTES:

STORAGE UNIT
CLEANOUT CHECKLIST

_____ Receipt with unit number and gate code

_____ Helpers (optional)

_____ Vehicle

_____ Masks (optional)

_____ Plastic Bags

_____ Gloves (optional)

_____ Dolly/Cart

_____ Water/Snacks (optional)

_____ Marker/Sharpie

_____ Personal items to office or left in unit with permission

_____ Box Cutter

_____ Broom & Dust pan

NOTES:

RESOURCES

www.wikipedia.org/wiki/self_storage

This site has a great history of the self-storage industry.

www.storagelaws.net

State by state lien laws related to self-storage, also some auction listings.

www.selfstorage.org

This site has news about the self-storage industry, their lobbying ability, and how to invest in a storage company.

www.storagelocations.com

Good for locating local self-storage facilities in your area.

www.storageauctions.com

At this site you pay for a list of storage auctions in California, it costs $155 per year and is only accurate to a point.

www.wastemanagement.com

Rentals for dumpsters, bins and containers, as well as, recycling scrap metal in California, Nevada, and Arizona.

www.secretsinstorage.com

If you have found the stories from storage in this book interesting you can check out our website for more stories and links to other sites that sell storage contents.

www.google.com

www.yahoo.com

These are both good search engines to use to research the name of a storage owner whose unit is coming up for auction. You can also locate local swap meets on this website by typing the name of the city and the word "swap meet."

WEBSITES FOR SELLING

www.iliadbooks.com

Sells used books and will buy them only if you bring them into the store, not over the internet.

www.half.com

Great to post used or new books and half.com pays twice per month with a deposit into your bank account.

www.amazon.com

Easy to post books CDs, DVDs. This site has a huge ISBN, bar code, and title search capacity, and it does sell other new items. Amazon.com also pays twice per month.

www.craigslist.com

Best for local sales and large items that need to be picked up. Very easy to post ads, place pictures and craigslist has a "free" category.

www.ebay.com

You can post your items auction style, buy it now or post them to an online eBay store. There are great tutorials available on eBay to help you post and sell on their site. EBay is a great place to research the price of an item you want to sell, just remember to always look at the completed sale price, not the listed price. To locate the following eBay sellers who post items bought at storage auctions, you need to click the advanced search icon on the eBay home page and type in search by seller name. (Note: to do an advanced search you must be an eBay member.)

Here some sellers I know: Auction-Buys-2009, Bob8311, Sharonsthriftstore (all one word), DizzyLiz9

SHIPPING

www.fedex.com

www.ups.com

www.usps.com

I use the post office for a number of reasons; the priority mail flat rate shipping boxes are a great value and media mail shipping for books, CDs, and DVDs is very reasonable. They have convenient locations. My post office knows me by name.

TRUCK RENTALS

www.uhaul.com

www.budgettruck.com

Budget costs more than U-Haul but their per mile charge is much less. Always remember to ask for a truck with a lift gate if you plan to empty a storage unit with lots of large items.

STORAGE FACILITIES: here's a list of the top five in the United States.

www.publicstorage.com

www.extraspacestorage.com

www.UstoreIT.com

www.sovanselfstorage.com - Uncle Bob's

www.uhaul.com/storage

If you need a storage unit for yourself in an emergency use Public Storage's dollar special. You will need to buy their lock and pay about $43 in other charges. If you move out in time and the unit stays vacant for seven days you usually can rent another unit for the dollar special. Many other storage facilities have specials and will usually rent to storage buyers.

PRECIOUS METALS

www.goldprice.com

Use this site to find the current price of pure gold, silver, or platinum per ounce.

www.dhfco.com

Use this site to sell scrap gold, other precious metals, and some electronics scrap.

FORMULAS

Formula for approximate price of scrap per gram of Gold/Silver/ Platinum

Gold - 14K

(Current price of gold) times .585 times .92 divided by 31.5 = price per gram

Gold - 18K

(Current price of gold) times .750 times .92 divided by 31.5 = price per gram

Gold - 10 K

(Current price of gold) times .415 times .92 divided by 31.5 = price per gram

Sterling Silver

(Current price of silver) times .925 times .92 divided by 31.5 = price per gram

(Current price of silver) times .925 times .92 = price per ounce

Platinum

(Current price of platinum) times .950 times .92 divided by 31.5 - price per gram

Please keep in mind that this is an approximate amount a buyer might pay for precious metal scrap. Also, keep in mind that finished jewelry with precious stones and antique jewelry may have more value than just the scrap metal price.

PAPERWORK EXAMPLES

Auction listing

Auction Sign-in Sheet

Storage Facility Map

Auction Receipt

Resale Certificate from California

Example 1: Auction listing

Bond #0434194
PHONE/Fax # (760)724-0423
westcoastauctions@gmail.com

WEST COAST AUCTIONS
2011 Nov. 2011

P.O. BOX 2071
Vista, Ca. 92085-2071

Nov. 7 At 10:00	Mon.	CANCELED	Linkletter Self Storage, 2318 E. South St., Long Beach approx. 8 units #(562)634-4084
Nov. 7 approx. 11:30			Extra Space Storage, 7471 Warner Ave., Huntington Beach approx. 6 units #(714)848-6572
Nov. 7 approx. 12:30			Extra Space Storage, 7531 McFadden Ave., Huntington Beach approx. 6 units #(714)895-7372
Nov. 7 approx. 1:30			Mini Public Self Storage, 11342 Western Ave., Stanton approx. 14 units (1) 12x15 full of ANTIQUES #(714)894-4724
Nov. 7 approx. 3:30		ADDED	Fast & Easy Storage, 5445 Olive St. , Montclair approx. 5 units #(909)985-9914
Nov. 8 At 9:00	Tue.		Sav-on Storage, 3712 Main Street, Chula Vista approx.10 units #(619)425-2040
Nov. 8 approx. 11:00			Secured Self Storage, 29135 Riverside Dr., Lake Elsinore approx. 7 units #(951)674-8681
Nov. 8 approx. 1:30			Extra Space Storage, 6942 Garden Grove Blvd., Westminster approx. 6 units #(714)897-6221
Nov. 8 approx. 2:00			Extra Space Storage,7392 Garden Grove Blvd., Westminster approx. 6 units #(714)898-2423
Nov. 8 approx. 3:30			Sun Valley Self Storage, 10991 Rosco Blvd., Sun Valley approx. 7 units #(818)768-1934
Nov. 9 At 8:30	Wed.		ACE Your Storage Place, 9672 Winter Gardens Blvd., Lakeside approx. 7 units #(619)443-9779
Nov. 9 approx. 9:30			ACE Your Storage Place, 573 Raleigh Ave., El Cajon approx. 6 units #(619)440-7867
Nov. 9 approx. 11:30		CANCELED	Extra Space Storage, 3881 Sherman St., San Diego approx. 12 units #(619)297-3503
Nov. 9 approx. 1:00			Extra Space Storage, 10115 Mission Gorge Rd., Santee approx. 7 units #(619)562-0101
Nov. 9 approx. 2:00			Extra Space Storage, 1539 E. Main St., El Cajon approx. 6 units #(619)401-0968
Nov. 9 approx. 3:00			Extra Space Storage, 8192 Miramar Rd./ Cabot, San Diego approx. 4 units #(858)549-2115
Nov. 9 approx. 3:30			Extra Space Storage, 8038 Arjons Dr., San Diego approx. 4 units #(858)549-8285
Nov. 9 approx. 4:00			Extra Space Storage, 6360 Miramar Rd., San Diego approx. 5 units #(858)453-3366
Nov. 10 At 8:30	Thur.		SOS Storage Centers, 31555 Canyon Estates Dr., Lake Elsinore approx. 5 units #(951)940-9990
Nov. 10 approx. 9:30			American Mini Storage, 41750 Rider Way, Temecula approx. 4 units #(951)676-4280
Nov. 10 approx. 10:30			Extra Space Storage, 372 W. Aviation Rd., Fallbrook approx. 5 units #(760)728-8267
Nov. 10 approx. 11:30			Extra Space Storage, 4705 N . River Rd., Oceanside approx. 8 units #(760)757-1225
Nov. 10 approx. 12:30			Extra Space Storage, 4567 Oceanside Blvd. Oceanside approx.10 units #(760)941-9401
Nov. 10 approx. 2:30		CANCELED	Bressi Ranch Self Storage, 2500 Campbell Place, Carlsbad approx. 5 units #(760)918-6600
Nov. 11 At 9:00	Fri.		StorQuest Self Storage, 83614 Dr. Carreon Blvd., Indio approx. 3 units #(760)863-1200
Nov. 11 approx. 9:30			StorQuest Self Storage, 47-250 Dune Palm Rd., La Quinta approx. 5 units #(760)777-1120
Nov. 11 approx. 11:00			Sure Save USA, 40050 Harris Ln., Palm Desert approx. 3 units #(760)200-9889

Example 2: Auction listing

DC#: 2156922

NOTICE OF PUBLIC SALE

Pursuant to the California Self-Service Storage Facility Act (B&P Code 21700 et seq.), the undersigned will sell at public auction, on **09/08/2011**, personal property including but not limited to furniture, clothing, tools and/or other household items located at:

PUBLIC STORAGE
PROPERTY 20435 @ 8:00 AM
18440 BURBANK BLVD
TARZANA, CA 91356-2802
(818) 881-1732
STORED BY THE FOLLOWING PERSONS:

5010 Steve Levy
1010 Barrington Hall
1108 Maria Taylor
1205 Kashmira Omar
2120 Samuel Cherry
2257 MANUCHEHR KARIMIRAD
2327 Robin Ballinger
2602 Veronica Lloyd
2703 Ali Ghazi
3442 Rolando Ramos
3548 Mitchell Bravo
4031 Jessica Acosta-Levy
5148 LINDA ELAMIN
6021 alex shapirshteyn
6426 Kecia Davis

PUBLIC STORAGE
PROPERTY 27311 @ 09:30 AM
19121 PARTHENIA STREET
NORTHRIDGE, CA 91324-3626
(818) 349-3173
STORED BY THE FOLLOWING PERSONS:

B010 TODD GALE
D029 Leslie Balta
D032 DEBORAH BEHRAD
D046 Taraneh Aliabadi
D086 Matt Magiera
D098 Irma Garcia
D109 Virgil Hood
D194 AMBER TOLSON
E100 JOSE ZAMORA
E240 ELIZABETH HILL
E242 DEBORAH SCOTT
E249 Chandra Chang
F022 Nathaniel Roberts

PUBLIC STORAGE
PROPERTY 20126 @ 10:30 AM
9341 SHIRLEY AVE
NORTHRIDGE, CA 91324-2489
(818) 772-4364
STORED BY THE FOLLOWING PERSONS:

1154 Brandon Nate
1222 margeurita Dancy
2093 DAVID ARMAS
2102 tim marion
2166 SHARI OSTER
2244 CAMILO ALLEN
2369 Kerri Farrands
2463 ERIC HAUCK
3027 ROGELIO NAVAR
3226 jackson mosley
3285 ROSA SANTILLAN
3376 JOSE GOMEZ
3424 DAVID CANCHOLA
3445 Kelly Ryan
B159 JUNNA NIWA
B258 Michael Phillips
B307 Eddina Jackson
C030 Michelle Werner
E250 CYNTHIA CAMPBELL
F012 DARRYL BRILLSON
H005 Larry Hainer
H090 ALYSAN ACHEN
H110 KAREN LENN
J006 ANGEL SALAZAR

PUBLIC STORAGE
PROPERTY 67676 @ 12:00 PM
18175 CHATSWORTH AVE
GRANADA HILLS, CA 91344-5613
(818) 832-2343
STORED BY THE FOLLOWING PERSONS:

B026 carol Littleford
B127 DOUGLAS GLEDHILL
B147 john pedraza
B210 MIGUEL PEREZ
B229 SANDRA BONAPARTE
C002 CHARLENE DECOFF
C027 jackie lutizetti
C033 Henry Nahabedian
C058 REBECCA BOTH
C108 Cesar Gonzalez

PUBLIC STORAGE
PROPERTY 08515 @ 1:00 PM
9920 BALBOA BLVD
NORTHRIDGE, CA 91325-1611
(818) 700-0698
STORED BY THE FOLLOWING PERSONS:

59 WILLIAM TRAUGER ,JR
2112 Cleon Jones
2212 EDUARDO VALDIVIA

PROPERTY 20630 @ 2:00 PM
8200 BALBOA BLVD
VAN NUYS CA 91406-1137
(818) 994-1511
STORED BY THE FOLLOWING PERSONS:

A005 CHARLIE EMFINGER
B016 Mark Lewis
C028 Destiny Saenz
C042 Mark Fenlason
C088 Daniel Delgado
C126 Gary Ananian
C174 Fernando Olaya
C226 LERNA TOUMAS
D307 David Banks
D447 Thomas King
D470 Voncille Williams
D516 Kathleen Ewing

PUBLIC STORAGE
PROPERTY 26311 @ 3:30 PM
7660 BALBOA BLVD
VAN NUYS, CA 91406-2297
(818) 994-6063
STORED BY THE FOLLOWING PERSONS:

A094 Shirley Stark
B011 Wendy Rector
D010 Naddia Pena
E042 Paul DiCocco
E063 Freddie Tiamzon
F111 Angel Monroe
G046 FRANK WILLIAMS
G053 David Gold
G071 Timothy Hill
G087 Heather Alsberg
G112 DAVID GOLD
P032 Karen Nazaryan
P034 Bags Costello

All sales are subject to prior cancellation. Terms, rules and regulations available at sale. Dated this **18th and 25th of August 2011** by PS Orangeco, Inc., 701 Western Ave., Glendale, CA 91201 (818) 244

Example 3: Auction Sign-in Sheet

Public Storage
The Real Storage Experts®

DELINQUENT TENANT SALE SIGN-IN SHEET AND AGREENEMNT

Property Name: ____________________ Property Number: ____________________

Date ____________________ Time ____________________

Rules and Regulations

1. All bidders must fill out the Bidders Sign-In Sheet (see below)
2. Purchaser must buy and remove everything in the space(s).
3. Contents must be removed from the space and property on the day of the sale unless otherwise specified by District Manager. however, purchaser must return photos, documents and other personal items to the property office.
4. Removal of goods is permitted only during posted office hours.
5. Purchaser forfeits all rights to all goods not removed within 48 hours and agrees such good may be resold or disposed without further notice to purchaser or refund of monies paid.
6. No Trash may be disposed in the Public Storage trash area.
7. All good sold "as is", there are no warranties or guarantees. Bids will be made based on visual inspection only. Bidders will not be allowed to handle goods or walk through the space(s) prior to sale.
8. Sale tax must be paid or purchaser must present completed Resale or Exemption Certificates for every unit they purchase. The signature on each certificate must be original and currently dated; no posted or predated certificates will be accepted.
9. Successful bidders may pay by money order, traveler's check, cash or credit card.
10. All high bids must be signed by the purchaser and their address, phone number, drivers license number and state of issuance must be indicated on the Certification of Public Sale form.
11. Zero buds must be signed by at least two bidders in attendance. Public Storage reserves the right to overbid, thus stopping the sale. Sales are not concluded until all paperwork is completed and tenant accounts are verified for any payments received prior sale.
12. The purchaser may not resale goods on the property
13. Any violation of the above rules may result in bidders being barred from future sale.
14. Public Storage reserves the right to null and void the auction and sale of any unit if, among other reasons, the District Manager verifies that the tenant has paid the outstanding balance in full while the auction was taking place.

BIDDER'S SIGN-IN SHEET		
Name (Please Print)	Signature	Telephone

Example 4: Auction Sign-in Sheet

TROJAN STORAGE

AUCTION TERMS & CONDITIONS

1. You must register to bid. A bidder must sign the auction sign in sheet
2. We reserve the right to refuse service to anyone at any time for any reason. Auctions are public, but do not guarantee that all the members of the public can participate
3. TERMS: CASH ONLY on award of bid. All units must be paid for immediately.
4. At discretion of Auctioneer, a minimum $50.00 refundable cleaning deposit per unit is required. CASH ONLY. The Auctioneer may charge a higher deposit on extra large units. Do not use the facility's dumpsters for trash. All items must be removed from the premises by 6pm tomorrow.
5. Bidder agrees, understands and abides by all rules and regulations posted by the facility. The Bidder shall have access to the facility and the unit only during posted office hours.
6. View units only from the door, and only in space designed by the Auctioneer. Do not break the plane of the door or touch any of the items in the units.
7. All units are sold "AS IS, WHERE IS." The Auctioneer, Facility Owner, Manager, or Agent makes no guarantees as to the contents of units. Box buyers: beware of the possibility that all boxes may be full of trash or empty. If so, they are still yours since unit is sold "AS IS." Newspaper legal ad may not agree with the goods in the unit. Do not speculate on what may be in the units.
8. All sales are final. No refunds, exchanges, or credits of any kind will be made.
9. **All personal papers (birth certificates, tax records, pictures, yearbooks, checking account information, etc.) found in storage unit should be returned to the storage company. If any of these terms are unacceptable or offensive to you, do not participate in the sale. All parties attending this sale are participating whether bidding or not.**
10. Bidder shall be responsible for anyone who is acting on behalf of bidder in any capacity and shall indemnify the storage facility, its Owner, Managers, and Agents, and Employees, etc. for any action whatsoever that may be born in any manner and hereby waive any claims against the storage facility. This waiver and responsibility shall also include any personal property damage, property damage to the self storage facility, its representatives, employees, occupants and customers.
11. The storage company is not responsible for losses due to fire, theft, vandalism, mysterious disappearances or any other events. Bidder shall provide insurance for losses incurred before, during and after sale.
12. The storage company reserves the right to bid.
13. The storage company reserves the right to hold any unit on a "contingent" basis at their sole and absolute discretion.
14. If any dispute arises, the resolution of the Auctioneer is final. Do not participate in this auction if you are not willing to accept the determination of the Auctioneer. By participating in this sale, you agree to abide by any and all Auctioneer's decisions.
15. Storage Company's liability for undeliverable units is limited to monies collected for purchase of unit(s) and cleaning deposit(s) only. The Auctioneer will make all reasonable efforts to deliver units to successful bidders. Bidder does not own these units until they are totally removed from the facility. The facility can claim units at any time without notice until they are totally removed. Any items that have been abandoned after seven days will be construed as abandoned property. Bidder will not be refunded bid price and/or cleaning deposit.
16. The ultimate responsibility of the unit being emptied and cleaned is that of the buyer. The buyer is responsible no matter what arrangements have been made to have the unit emptied. Legal action will be taken against the buyer for costs and/or time involved in cleaning any debris left behind.

The undersigned hereby agrees that the terms and conditions above and on the reverse side are incorporated as part of the Auction Terms & Conditions.

SIGNATURE: Sharon Pereira **Print Name** SHARON PEREIRA **Date:** 11-16-11

Example 5: Storage Facility Map

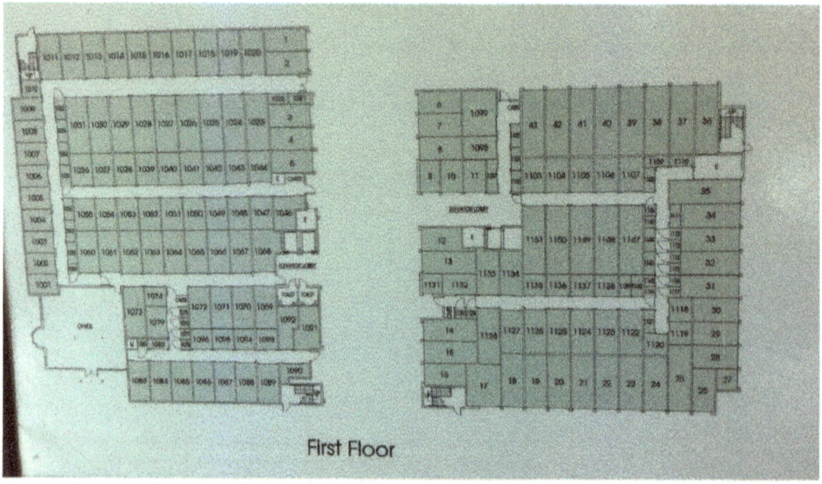

* 555666 # Temp Exc

Public Storage
Problem Solved

CERTIFICATION OF PUBLIC SALE

PROPERTY #/ADDRESS: 16400 Foothill Blvd. Tujunga Ca 91042

The goods, chattels or personal property stored as indicated below are being sold pursuant to the Self-Service Storage Statute for the State of: Calif

Space: B028 Tenant Name: Leonardo Ramirez

1. I hereby certify that I bid/offer $ 25 cash to purchase the contents of the storage space identified above and certify that my bid was made at competitive bidding during which competitive bids were made by other parties and entertained by PS Orangeco, Inc., and that my bid was the highest and winning bid.

   D.L.# N4010430 State CA

   By: Sharon Pereida Address: 8381 San Fernando Rd

   Phone: 818-492-7841 Sun Valley Ca 91352

2. I/We hereby certify that I/we offered Zero Dollars ($0.00) for the contents of the storage space identified above, in bid(s) made at competitive bidding; no other bidder would offer any money for the above identified storage space and that in my/our opinion its contents have no value. (Note: A minimum of three (3) signatures required.)

   Name: ______ Name: ______

   Name: ______ Name: ______

3. I promise to abide by Public Storage's Rules and Regulations as set forth in the Delinquent Tenant Sale Sign-In Sheet and Agreement.

4. I promise to return all photos, documents (e.g., birth certificates and passports), and other personal items ("Personal Property") to the property office. I also agree to indemnify, defend, and hold harmless Public Storage and the owner of the facility for all claims and demands relating to the Personal Property.

5. I understand that Public Storage reserves the right to null and void the auction and sale of the unit for any reason.

Date of Sale: 9/21/11 By: Sharon Pereida
Purchaser
Printed Name: SHARON PEREIDA

BILL OF SALE

DATE: 11/8/11 UNIT NO.: E 023 LESSEE: ______

PRICE: 25.00 RESALE NO.: ______

TAX: 0 CLEANING DEPOSIT: $40.00

TOTAL: 25.00 DEPOSIT REFUNDED: ______

All purchases are as is, where is. No warranties expressed or implied as to fitness or saleability.

Anything not removed by 5:30, on 11/9/11 from premises shall be deemed abandoned unless other arrangements have been made with management.

SELLER: ______ BUYER: ______

OWNER/AGENT FOR: ADDRESS: ______

SUN VALLEY SELF STORAGE
10991 Roscoe Boulevard
Sun Valley, CA 91352

PHONE: ( ) ______

AUCTIONEER: ______ STATE LICENSE #: 0434194

P.O. Box 2071 PHONE: (760) 724-0423

Vista, CA 92085

Example 6: Auction Receipt

CASHIER SYSTEM * * * CASH RECEIPT * * *

Receipt # 580543

Receipt Date: 10/06/11 2:56pm

SA Recycling LLC
8250 Tujunga Ave.
Sun Valley, CA 91352
(818) 767-4388

RC 14566

Purchased From: NEW000
WHATS NEW
8311 SAN FERNADO RD.
LP#UV55115
SUN VALLEY, CA 91352

Ticket#	Ship Dt	Commodity	Price UM	Frt Ext	Total Amt
TDUSHD	10/06/11	METAL	340.0000 GT	0.00	355.16
		Veh#: TK 5U59449	Weights: 14880g	12540t	2340n
ZDYCSG	10/06/11	#2 COPPER	2.1500 LB	0.00	25.80
		Veh#: TK	Weights: 72g	60t	12n
ZDYCSG	10/06/11	#2 ICW 50%	1.1000 LB	0.00	39.60
		Veh#: TK	Weights: 264g	228t	36n
ZDYCSG	10/06/11	BRASS-YELLOW	1.8000 LB	0.00	106.20
		Veh#: TK	Weights: 62g	3t	59n
ZDYCSG	10/06/11	ALUM PAINTED OLD SHE	0.5500 LB	0.00	2.75
		Veh#: TK	Weights: 12g	7t	5n
ZDYCSG	10/06/11	ZINC DIE CAST IRONY	0.1800 LB	0.00	2.16
		Veh#: TK	Weights: 19g	7t	12n
ZDYCSG	10/06/11	ELECTRIC MOTORS	0.2500 LB	0.00	25.50
		Veh#: TK	Weights: 228g	126t	102n
Supplier NEW000 Totals (Pounds):			15537g	12971t	2566n

TOTAL AMOUNT PAID TO SUPPLIER (CASH): $557.17

Cashier Signature ______________________
(Laura Lopez)

Customer Signature ______________________

(All weights are reported in Pounds unless otherwise indicated)
(All non-Pound weights are assumed to be manual weights)
(a=Scale 1 b=Scale 2 c=Scale 3 d=Scale 4 m=Manual Weight)

any issues or concerns please contact our customer service dept.
(800) GOT-SCRAP

Customer C...

BOE-230 (7-02)
GENERAL RESALE CERTIFICATE

STATE OF CALIFORNIA
BOARD OF EQUALIZATION

California Resale Certificate

I HEREBY CERTIFY:

1. I hold valid seller's permit number: ______________________

2. I am engaged in the business of selling the following type of tangible personal property:

____

3. This certificate is for the purchase from ______________________ [Vendor's name] of the item(s) I have listed in paragraph 5 below.

4. I will resell the item(s) listed in paragraph 5, which I am purchasing under this resale certificate in the form of tangible personal property in the regular course of my business operations, and I will do so prior to making any use of the item(s) other than demonstration and display while holding the item(s) for sale in the regular course of my business. I understand that if I use the item(s) purchased under this certificate in any manner other than as just described, I will owe use tax based on each item's purchase price or as otherwise provided by law.

5. Description of property to be purchased for resale:

6. I have read and understand the following:

For Your Information: A person may be guilty of a misdemeanor under Revenue and Taxation Code section 6094.5 if the purchaser knows at the time of purchase that he or she will not resell the purchased item prior to any use (other than retention, demonstration, or display while holding it for resale) and he or she furnishes a resale certificate to avoid payment to the seller of an amount as tax. Additionally, a person misusing a resale certificate for personal gain or to evade the payment of tax is liable, for each purchase, for the tax that would have been due, plus a penalty of 10 percent of the tax or $500, whichever is more.

NAME OF PURCHASER

SIGNATURE OF PURCHASER, PURCHASER'S EMPLOYEE OR AUTHORIZED REPRESENTATIVE

PRINTED NAME OF PERSON SIGNING	TITLE

ADDRESS OF PURCHASER

TELEPHONE NUMBER	DATE
( )	

Some Frequently Asked Questions

1. Can anyone buy at a storage auction? Yes, unless you have been banned from the property. Remember though, you must have funds available before you bid.

2. Are they all cash sales? Almost all storage facilities in Los Angeles sell at auction on a cash only basis. A few that I know of, Public Storage included, accept credit cards. Be sure to find out whether you need cash or can use a credit card before you sign up to bid.

3. What size vehicle will I need? The bigger the better! Storage units can be packed so tight that it's hard to imagine how the previous owner got everything in. If you plan on loading up a pick up be sure to have tie downs. Bring help with you to load the stuff.

4. What if the auctioneer doesn't acknowledge my bid? Most auction buyers speak up or raise their hands to be obvious. Stand close to the auctioneer so he can hear or see you if you want to bid on the unit and are concerned that they may not see you.

5. Can I rent the storage unit that I buy if I need to? Yes, many times you can; it depends on the auctioneer and property manager.

6. What was the oddest, best, and worst items you found in storage? I believe the oddest two items I found in storage were a tesslor coil that I thought was a homemade bomb and a big ladies prosthetic left leg size 10. The best thing I found, other than the cash and coins that I frequently find, was a two-ounce square of pure gold, which sold for $1000 per ounce at the time. The worst item was a two-gallon gas can full of urine with a sock for a cap.

Intermedia Publishing Group

Do you need a speaker?

Do you want Sharon Pereida to speak to your group or event? Then contact Larry Davis at: **(623) 337-8710** or email: **ldavis@intermediapr.com** or use the contact form at: **www.intermediapr.com**.

Whether you want to purchase bulk copies of *Storage Units* or buy another book for a friend, get it now at: **www.imprbooks.com**.

If you have a book that you would like to publish, contact Larry Davis, Publisher, at Intermedia Publishing, (623) 337-8710 or email: **ldavis@intermediapr.com** or use the contact form at: www.intermediapub.com.